John R. Effinger.

March. } Baltimore
1863. } Md.

BY THE SAME AUTHOR.

THE PATIENCE OF HOPE.

1 volume. 16mo. $1.00.

A PRESENT HEAVEN.

ADDRESSED TO A FRIEND.

1 volume. 16mo. $1.00.

In Press.

POEMS,

BY THE SAME AUTHOR.

TICKNOR AND FIELDS, Publishers.

Two Friends

BY

THE AUTHOR OF "THE PATIENCE OF HOPE"
AND "A PRESENT HEAVEN"

ET TENEO ET TENEOR

BOSTON
TICKNOR AND FIELDS
1863

AUTHOR'S EDITION.

University Press:
Welch, Bigelow, and Company,
Cambridge.

DEDICATED

TO

THOMAS CONSTABLE

BY HIS ATTACHED FRIEND

THE AUTHOR.

October 7th, 1862.

"Meanwhile the gold King was asking the man, 'How many secrets knowest thou?' 'Three,' replied the man. 'Which is the most important?' said the silver King. '*The open one,*' replied the other. 'Wilt thou open it to us also?' said the brass King. '*When I know the fourth!*' replied the man."

"Have we not all one Father? hath not one God created us? *And did not he make one?*" — MALACHI ii. 10, 15.

TWO FRIENDS.

I WAS born beneath quiet hills, among green pastures, beside still waters. My first companion was a little stream, my earliest counsellor an ancient book. Along the edge of the stream ran a footpath, so narrow, so rarely trodden, that the ferns and wild-flowers would sometimes overgrow and even hide it; and then the brook itself became my guide: one that I followed confidingly, because I knew and loved it under every change. It would sometimes so contract the channel of its hurrying waters as to leave a broad pebbly shingle, warm in the blaze of noonday, and friendly to my childish feet. The trees which fringed it on either side would now interlace their boughs so closely that I could scarcely push my way between them, and they would now recede, opening out some little bay of verdure, some green savanna which had been cleared of its thick nut-bushes and clinging brambles, and from whence, through the trees that still held it in their arms, one might gain a sunny reach of corn-field, a glimpse of some distant village, and see, beyond all, a low range of hills that seemed to bound the prospect, and yet to hide, to promise nothing. I dwelt long beside the little stream; so long, that the seasons above me changed greatly, the dark thunder-cloud broke above me, the drenching shower fell, the frost set in that is too intense to be searching, when Nature's heart dies within her, and makes no sign. By the banks of that little brook, Trouble overtook me. Pain — at whose breath the flowers paled, the green leaves shrunk up, and fell upon the ground fire-smitten — led me long time by the hand. Even Anguish met me; but never Discord. My way might be steep and unalluring; but it was always plain, "straight as a line could make it," and tending to a foreseen, though distant end. My heart was troubled, but unresisting; so methought He bringeth them to the haven where they would be. The birds sang to me at morn and even; at morn and even I read within my book. How was it that the brook suddenly became wider; that it swelled into a mighty river; that the trees upon its banks grew thick and tangled, and spread into broad, untracked woods; while far behind, in place of the low hills, that were but the plain raised to a higher level, rose mountains with cloven summits, down which the clouds stole. They beckoned me to them with a lure, a promise: it was not, I knew, for nothing that they lifted themselves thus proudly into heaven; that they sank their firm foundations so deep within the earth, placing themselves among the things that cannot be shaken. I had heard, of old, this saying, "The mountains shall bring peace." O that I could reach unto them! that I might gaze from their glorious peaks! that I might delve within their unsunned mines! and I struck within the forest by many paths, but without finding that which led to the mountains.

One day, after a long breathing pause, I again pressed onward. Suddenly parting the boughs, I came upon the ruins of an ancient temple; its white shafts rose against the dark forest background, and still, in their broken outline, preserved the trace of the building's original plan, as a lovely, once-heard tune will return upon the ear in fragments, and hint out its half-forgotten melody. Bright trailing weeds crept up these broken pillars. Here and there a statue still stood erect, — still breathed with a divine impassive life; and some, fallen and mutilated, lay among the warm grass; but these, too, *lived;* these too, methought, triumphed, for their smile still made silence eloquent. Who were these forms? the sons of strength and beauty, of light and freedom, — the children of some golden, untrammelled age, unfettered, godlike? If sleeping they could thus stir, thus enchain the soul, what had they been in their waking? What was this pride upon their lips, this calm, this sweetness of their brows? What had *my* life been, how poor, how restricted, that even the dream of such forms had never visited it; that the shadow of their wings had never fallen across my sleep, the bright curve of their half-parted lips never greeted my waking? A cold gnawing fell upon my heart; a scorn, that was almost hate of things familiar and accustomed, and of the life that had been passed among them. Had this indeed been *life?*

While I asked myself this question, music awoke around me. I listened: it was high noon: the birds were silent in the forest; the shattered columns, the fair-gleaming statues, stood up clear against the broad depth of the summer heaven. Not a breeze rustled, not a leaf shook. Yet around, above, within me, that music gathered; it grew stronger in the silence; it bore me up as on mighty wings; it carried me I knew not whither; in a moment of time it had taught me the secret of a hundred hearts, — tears and raptures, despairs and exultations, too mighty for one bounded spirit. It gathered all things within it, as a mother might draw her erring, repentant children unto her bosom; making room for deep confessions, for reconciliations that were still more ample. Here, too, were recognitions of wide relationships, affinities disowned and slighted, that only could meet and kiss each other for a moment while the pitying music sobbed above them. And still the strain awoke and died; still it returned upon itself, as friends, who, meeting after long parting, must again part, come back again with some word that can never be fully spoken. It went forth, it returned, then with a firm, soft clasp, as of a little child's hand, it clasped the spirit closely; it held Earth compressed in a little space; it brought down Heaven to a point of ecstasy.

I fled from it; I struggled to regain the river; I forced my way back through the thick odor-breathing trees, through the wreaths, the ropes of flowers that hung from them, and sought to stay me in their twining arms. Were these, too, conspirators, the purple and scarlet blossoms, that breathed out their heavy hearts, full of anguish and of love, so that I seemed, as I tore my way through them, to drink in their fiery and fragrant souls. — Are there, I asked, martyrs among the flowers? spirits burning, yet unconsumed, that light up their own lives! The strife, the revel of the music, had passed within them; they glowed, they paled with its triumph and its decline. Like moons, they filled themselves with light at its fountain; their hues, their odors, were in secret, deep alliance with its choral mystery. Here, too, were subtle interfusions; sudden, yet long-anticipated climaxes of splendor; discords that prophesied the harmony they seemed to contradict; laws broken, to be fulfilled in a deeper spirit.—At length I regained the river, but not at the point where I had left it; at a little distance it lay before me like a glittering bow, flung down amid the woods that swept back from it in broad, smooth masses. A little lower down, I saw that the words were broken by huge masses of rock, now reddening in the westering sun, and I heard a hoarse murmur, as of water, that chafed within a narrowed channel; but at the spot where I now stood, all was peace and loveliness. The river looked like a lake, so broad was it, so serene, so unruffled; it spread its calm bosom to the evening sky; the clouds saw themselves within it like islets of floating flame. It curved gently to my feet, as if it would woo me also to linger. Peace, peace, it whispered; wilt thou not also rest? the evening bringeth all things home.

But even as it were half consciously I went still onward, and drew gradually more near the rocks. As I approached still nearer, a strong slanting beam from the red sunset fell across them for a moment, and I saw that they were scored all over with Runic characters. These, I thought, contain the history of some vanished people, — some race passed by, like a wave or a cloud, for ever; but, lo! as I set my heart to interpret these mystic traceries, I found that they were but a long, unbroken family tradition, the story of the Many and the One, the life of Man. These rocks drew me to them with an iron magnetism; I lived, I slept beneath them; morn and even I pored upon their records till all their subtle symbolism grew familiar to me, as to a child the pictures upon the walls of his nursery. I stood beside the cradles of giant nations; I listened to the songs that were sung, the legends that were told to races in their mighty youth. They changed often, yet they were still sweet, still intelligible; *for they were the same songs sung by the same cradle, the same stories told beside the same hearth.* Through them all ran one device, as of two arrows so closely bound together that they seemed one. The arrow was borne onwards by the song, the song sharpened by the arrow; each pointed to an age far back in dim perspective, when gods walked on earth, and earth was worthy of their footprints; each pointed, though darkly, to a return of this period; a return only to be achieved through voluntary, self-chosen pain, and the suffering of that which is divine.

Then these songs of sadness and of glory ceased, or came across the ear fitfully, as music might come across a stormy and bitter wave. I saw generations of men crowd and press upon each other; as the worm toils beneath the Southern Ocean, so they toiled in countless myriads from birth even unto death, building up their lives within the fabric of some giant despotism. Behold, what manner of stones, and what buildings are these, and within them a mummy or an ape in effigy! Then, as a mighty inundation breaks down the thick-woven jungle, snaps its tall reeds, lays bare the haunts of the wild forest-dwellers, and hurries down to the sea with the lion and the lamb, the snake and the antelope, creatures deadly and innocent, floating on its swift current, hurled to one common ruin, so came the fresh tide of men: by land and by sea they came; swift, compact, irresistible, bearing down all before them. I heard their wild chants, their shouts of pride and triumph:

> "We have sung them the Mass of Lances,
> It lasted from morning till sunset.
>
> . . . . .
>
> The might of the tempest is the strength of the rower,
> It does but carry us where we wish to go."

Yet slowly, from amidst these wrecks, rose up the old foundations, the strongholds of greed and cruelty; their stones were welded together firmly as at the first, and cemented as at the first with the sweat of man's brow, the life-blood of his heart. I saw the people strong and patient; an ass that stooped down between two burdens, accustomed to the yoke from youth, yet sometimes striking out fiercely with its iron-shod hoofs. I saw the human heart made the football of tyrants, the plaything of cruel children, who knew not the excellence of that with which they sported. I saw it defrauded both of its highest and its humblest hopes; cheated alike out of its birthright and its pottage; sold in the market-place and in the temple; its dearest interests set upon a cast of dice, or bartered for the cold smile of a wanton. Yea, more than this, I saw a Terror that had crept within the souls of men. A divine voice had once spoken: "Fear ye not them which kill the body, and after that have no more that they can do." Shall man be free within his own spirit; free to love and pray, to call upon God in his own language? Here also shall man be a slave; when the hunters are upon him, let him not think to cross this boundary: it exists no longer. Two dark tyrannies, stretching till they meet, have taken in man's whole being. If he would mount up into heaven, it is there; if he would lie down in the grave, it is there also:

chains, darkness, the gripe of the unrelenting bloodhound. I saw a foreground of desolation, a background of abject terror, lit up with ghastly fires. I saw Humanity stand within the world's judgment-hall, gagged, insulted, with its hands bound behind it, the scoff of Soldier and of Priest, yet at that moment I heard the voice of one that spake, low but distinct, from amid the torture, "*Eppure si muove*," and I saw that the soul *grew*. Bound even with a band of brass and iron,* it lay yet in the tender grass of the field, it was yet wet with the dew of heaven. From time to time some heart, within which the fire had long smouldered, would break and go out, it seemed in ashes and darkness, yet those fiery sparks had made the darkness visible; no longer was it such as could be felt. Then light arose, but with it came confusion; the heart was no longer trampled on, but it erred, it was the robber of its own wealth.

Then I remembered the saying of the wise man, "That which is wanting cannot be numbered." I thought I will read no longer; these

* Daniel iv. 23.

records are too sorrowful; there is surely a less perplexing lore. I will seek out the broad, loving secret of the universe; I will decipher its clear story, not blurred and defeatured like this one, but as it lies before me in the original handwriting of God. But in this attempt also was anguish. When I flung myself on Nature's broad bosom for comfort, its coldness stung me like a thorn; there was no warm, tender heart within it to respond to my own that beat so wildly; its pulsation was that of a vast machinery, life and death that sprung out of each other, all things bound in order, in fatality; a Universe that ground upon its way, sowing the Expanse with worlds as its fiery sparks flew off. Here I saw splendor and desolation, as of a magnificent household, lavish in its expenditure, because its resources are illimitable. What meant these monkeys that grinned and chattered; these snakes with their cold crowns and glittering eyes; the rustle of the fierce and lovely leopard? Also the flowers put on a look of mockery; their aspects revealed strange affinities, awoke suggestions of doubtful import.

Were these house-children also wicked and guileful? Was there treachery in this broad, universal calm of Nature, in this impassive smile that, sphinx-like, told nothing and hid so much? As I pursued her she still fled before me, still flung me from time to time, half derisively, some intricate toy, a golden apple that did but stay me from the final goal. Then, as if in sleep or death, she would stretch herself before me in a feigned immobility, wrapped in a thousand folds; and when I pierced beneath one, beneath a hundred, there was still another and another. Were these swaddling-clothes or grave-bands? I knew not. Here I found design, I knew not to what end; power; here also *bondage* more cruel, I thought, than that of men over their fellows, for the heart that has fallen under it has no escape; *it is coextensive with the universe itself.* I sat down, a stone among the stones; let the seasons roll, I would grow gray like them, and motionless. My eye wandered listlessly over the gorgeous landscape, the little islets of white sculptured lilies, the purple woods, the far-distant mountains. Here was a magnificent panorama of death, a shining veil drawn over a face that writhed in anguish.

Then, upon a rock above me, my eye lit upon a familiar sign, a cross, and beneath it these letters, —

"Vis fugere a Deo, fuge ad Deum,"

and while I gazed, a pale majestic face looked upon me rebukingly; a form passed by, with kingly but uneven step, as of one wounded even to death. He spoke not, but I read within his eye this saying, "*Faithful are the wounds of a friend.*" Then I sighed within my spirit so deeply that an icy band burst; resistance, rebellion, were gone. The yoke to which God himself had stooped could not be too grievous to be borne. I saw this solemn Trinity, Nature and Man and God, pierced with the self-same wound. I knew that they would suffer, I knew that they would be restored together. Where was now the cold sequence, the crushing, unpitying regularity? Let the worlds roll together, let the heavens and the earth be changed, Jesus, thou, too, art part of God's mighty plan! I sat down beneath this rock, not elate, but satisfied; its broad shadow fell over me; from beneath it I gazed upon the dark woods, the fair river. Once again I looked up to that Sign of love and triumph; then I observed that it was green; some soft bright lichen had sown itself within the deep-cut symbol, and a prophetic word fell upon my spirit: "The dry tree shall flourish"; the cross also shall become green, shall be vivified with the heart it vivifies.

I arose and went forward, so sunk in thought that I did not see that as I went on the river shrunk gradually till it was scarcely broader than it had been in olden days; it grew narrower and narrower; rocks shut it in on either side, sometimes dipping clear into the water so as to leave no foot-way, sometimes sending out a wide stony strand which seemed to press the contracted current out of life; vexed and tortured, it revenged itself by wearing caverns beneath the stone where it whirled in still black pools unseen for ever. The trees, the flowers, were left far behind; the river had grown sombre and taciturn. O, how I missed its early cheerfulness, the nut and alder bushes that overhung its banks; the scarlet berry of the mountain-ash in autumn, the white stain of the wild cherry-tree in spring; the leap of the trout, the glimmer of the dragon-fly, the brown wet shine of the smooth stones beneath the stream. I thought of the unequal stepping-stones, inviting to a perilous joy; the frequent bridge, rustic and tremulous, upon which it was so sweet to linger, to cross and recross without any stringent motive. Then the little brook had been companionable, garrulous; it chode, it murmured incessantly, yet said nothing; it did not need to speak articulately, for it was in accordance with all that surrounded it. What need for speech or language where a Voice was ever heard?

Then, too, I had had many companions, playmates, and work-fellows, whose looks, whose voices had been dearer to me than aught by the brook or in the forest. Sometimes we had read together in the book; sometimes we had knelt and prayed together in the clear evening light.

We loved each other; we shared together many innocent secrets, many joys and tears, many thoughts that we passed, as in a torch-race, from hand to hand; the light that dawned upon one heart would grow to-day in another. I thought it would be thus for ever. Had these deserted me, or had *I* left them, ever following the course of this mysterious river? Their voices sounded clear and cold, like distant bells, tender only through some long-past association. Even those of my beloved Dead were nearer; but *these*, too, had grown thin as the music of the wind-swept pine-tree. *I knew that I was now alone.* I could not reunite these ties; I could not bring back the Past, which had gone for ever. It was not night within my soul, for neither moon nor stars appeared; no soft lure held me back; no bright, unsteadfast hope urged me forward. Neither found I the blackness of darkness within my spirit, but a strange freedom, joined with a loneliness that was almost fearful. Around, within me was calm, and silence that spread and stretched like the desert, ever widening, to widen ever; a grave that was shut in by no bars. "Free," I said, "among the dead." Like one continually ascending, I had left the pale saxifrage, the last flower that fringes the verge of ice, behind me. The air grew keen and difficult. Every step revealed some fresh undreamt-of glory, some rose-flushed summit, some meeting-ground of earth and heaven; but it was chill; I drew my breath with pain; my heart seemed to have ceased beating, but when I laid my hand upon it, I found that it burned with self-fed, self-centred fire.

Then, suddenly, there fell upon my soul a sense of greatness, telling me to be no more sorrowful, for that I was not really alone, but part of a Whole in which I should find all things, — those that I had left behind, those that I had failed to reach to, yea, my own life also. If it be indeed so, I thought, then I refuse not to die; to lose that which is in part, in the coming in of that which is perfect. But how may my spirit attain unto this baptism? Oftentimes I seemed near some mighty secret, to lie on the very threshold of Truth; *but to be chained there:* a spell was upon that threshold that never allowed me to overpass it. On the flower, the shell, the wing of the butterfly, were traces of a writing whose counterpart was in my own soul; as when a page has been torn down the midst, I found I had only to join these characters to make their meaning plain. The winds, the leaves, my own voice and that of the birds, were harmony; I strove to master it; to pierce to its deep fundamental structure. Then the rocks began to give forth music at sunrise and sunset; not like that alluring, bewildering music of the forest and ruined temple, but solemn and chastened. *That* sweetness dissolved the spirit; this built it up within its mighty chord. Each scattered drop, each bright spark of melody that had fallen here and there, making some stray blade or blossom lovely, shone there, gathered up into a lofty arch of sound that might grow, I thought, to one of Triumph, spanning earth and heaven. It was ever pure, ever prophetic; yet now, as I listened, it seemed to me that there were but two who spake within it, exchanging, as in some old, simple song, the

I and *Thou* of an unalterable constancy; then it would grow to the voice of a great multitude, to the sound of many waters. I heard harpers harping on their harps, compassing me about with songs of deliverance; and yet the music did not change.

For hours I would lie listening to the birds; for hours I would toil among the flowers and fossils I had collected; once more I read at morn and even in my book. Then as I lay at midday, a light above the brightness of the noon would sometimes be cast around me, and a well-known Form would pass me, as one in haste. His step was still regal; his garments red, from the battle or the vintage, I knew not which; but his eye was calm as that of one who follows out some vast, long-deliberated plan. He did not stay to speak with me, but in passing me his step was slower, and once he turned and looked upon me for a moment. I understood that silent appeal, yet I did not respond to it, did not follow where it led. I had experienced, endured so much; weariness of all things, even of good, had overtaken me; a spring in my life that kept all moving had run low, had stopped altogether. Then understood I why a certain Father had said, "I have written unto *you*, young men, *because ye are strong*." Even now, far above the valley, I heard the clear songs of the vintagers, the shouts of those who carried home the corn; the fields stood white, all things told me that the Harvest of the earth had come, and its Lord would immediately thrust in the sickle. How gladly would I once have joined these bands, have shared in their labors, their rewards! I thought of the plans I had formed with my old play-fellows, how we would clear jungles, would found villages; now I had ceased to plan, perhaps because I had ceased to hope. How, too, could I leave this world so lately found, so hardly won; too late I loved thee, thou fair, ever-changing realm of Nature! This high rock-girdled paradise of thought and beauty, this citadel of refuge, this green enclosure, — *is it not a little one?* passed by by the busy foot, overlooked by the curious eye, fair only to the heart that loves it, yet hard to leave. I know thee, Jesus, that thou art an hard man, reaping where thou hast not sown, gathering where thou hast not strawed. I remembered one who had gone away sorrowful because he had *a small possession*, and I felt that the full hand has the loosest grasp. The withered tendrils cling closer than the green; when the rose was yet heavy with dew, and fragrance, it had not been so hard to pluck it off!

And that benignant form still passed upon his way, still looked upon me in sadness, but without austerity. Jesus, thou knowest the heart, but thou art greater than our heart, and knowest all things! The Poor committeth himself unto Thee.

One day I had turned aside to track the course of a little brawling stream that fell into the river; its waters were of a clear golden brown, like that of the dying fern; it had come across many a lonely moor from the mountains, and might, I thought, take me with it to its birthplace. First, however, it led me into a still gray valley, strewn with pieces of rock, that looked at a little distance like a flock of sheep feeding, and added to the peaceful charm of the scene. All breathed security. I wandered to and fro without much thought; I threw myself upon the warm grass, resting my head upon one of the gray stones. It was Autumn, one of those days that are sweeter, kinder than the Spring. The wind blew strong, yet softly; it wakened I know not what echoes among the rocks, the mountains, yet within the valley all was still; the birches that hung from its rocky sides scarcely shook; only from time to time a thrill as of pleasure passed through them. Often have I listened to the wind with rapture, but never did it bear to me so full, so rich a message, one of unspeakable tranquillity, and hope so calm, that I knew not whether this voice came to me out of the past or out of the future; all that was sweet, was desired in either, seemed to mingle in it. Can ecstasy, I thought, wear such sober colors? A Hand seemed to guide that rushing wind; it fell upon my cheek, my forehead, like a blessing warm from some heart of more than human tenderness. Then my own heart stirred and fluttered beneath that brooding warmth, and from its very depths two words went up, "Our Father," and I knew that I had found the long-sought key, the pure, primeval language. This then was what I sought, what I needed, a Father who was a Spirit, the Father of Spirits and of men. *Had he indeed come forth to meet me? Then I knew that I was not far from home.*

"I shall rest," I said, "beneath His wings, and I shall be safe among His feathers." A calm of feeling fell upon me, such as is wont to precede the great crises of life, when the soul, feeling itself upon the very threshold of a new existence, is held back there by the old one, which, before it is left behind forever, has many things to say, and concentrates its spirit within a few solemn moments:—

"Last night I saw the new moon,
With the old moon in her arms."

There are some days, even moments, in our lives, *upon which the burden of the whole seems laid*, which, as in a parable, condense within them the mystery, the contradiction of our existence, and *perhaps hint at its solution.* After such times, life grows clearer before and after.

These seasons are set apart from the rest by a solemn consecration. We feel that we are anointed "above our fellows"; it may be for the joy of the bridal, for the wrestler's struggle, *or against the day of our burial*, we know not which.

The mountain stream had become a friend to me; its voice reminded me of that of my earliest companion, the brook, in the days when we had been young together. The noon drew to its decline, filling the glen with a calm golden light, that, meeting with its own lustre on the fading leaves, kindled them into a sudden radiance. I followed the stream slowly, when, as it were, in a moment, it ended, and the valley with it. It was as if the craggy, woody ledge of a mountain had slipt forward, and brought the scene to a close so abruptly that one might think there was nothing beyond, and that the world itself ended here. Yet the stream gave this thought a joyous contradiction as it fell from height to height, flashing lightly between the bushes that half hid it, and gathering itself at the foot of the rock into a deep unsunned pool. Looking closer, too, I saw a steep path, by which an agile climber might wend his way up the rock without much difficulty; but I at that moment felt in no mood for adventure. I stood long, half listening to the falling water, half gazing at the singular, enchanting scene; when far above me I heard a clear, low whistle, and, looking up, saw the brown, handsome face of one who bent over the crag, and nodded to me, as if in recognition.

I smiled in return, for the loneliness drew us together like a band.

He called to me, "Shall I show you the upward path?" I shook my head; so, half leaping from point to point, half swinging himself from bough to bough, using both feet and hands freely, he let himself down the rock, and soon reached the place where I was standing. Then I saw that his dress was plain, even to homeliness, yet his air was free and noble; he set his foot firmly on the ground, as one who found his place wherever he happened to stand. In all his movements there was a decision, a rapidity, that made, as it were, a wind that carried him forward; a light, pleasant rustling, a joyous excitement, as of the chase or the voyage, seemed to follow where he went. But did I see this at first! did I see anything in thee at first and at last but thy kindness, Philip! From the first unto the last thou wert unto me a friend; one that showed himself friendly.

He saw that I looked wearied, and offered me a cordial from a flask that he carried with him. As he poured it out, the wind blew aside his vest, and I saw that he carried within his bosom the book that had so long been my companion. We sat together on the trunk of a fallen tree; we talked till the shadows began to gather round us thickly. The dying light, the faint shiver of the leaves above us, the mystery, the solitude that enclosed us, — all seemed to exalt, to deepen our converse, to shorten our way into each other's hearts, by removing all that ofttimes drops like a veil between soul and soul, changing us from our truer, better selves in an evil transfiguration. But had I met thee, Philip, in the thick of this world's conventions, even there, even at first meeting, we had made for ourselves a solitude, like this one, populous with thought.

I asked him many questions about the mountains, about the broad plains of toil and conflict that spread below them, on which I found he was a dweller. Then, in return, he inquired eagerly into the secrets of the broad river, the rocks, the forest. I found they were not unknown ground to him, though their spells had never laid so strong a grasp on his spirit as on mine. "For I," he said, smiling, "came not in by the Gate which is called Beautiful." He examined my store of specimens with eager curiosity. My own spirit caught the flame, each withered flower seemed to bloom, each pebble to flash like an opal, as I spread them forth before him. They had never before seemed so valuable to me, yet I exclaimed, with a hasty impulse, "Take any of them, all; you will use, enjoy them; I perhaps have done neither."

"Nay," he returned, laughing, "the best things are those which are shared, not given. I will take nothing from you; for a gift demands a gift in return, and what have I to give you in exchange? Nothing."

"Nothing," I answered him, "except that which is the fibre and soul of all things,— Hope."

"Well, then," he said, looking at me with his clear, honest eyes, "I will make a good bargain, and traffic with that against your wisdom."

I laughed in my turn, and said, "Agreed, if you will exchange that word for my experience."

"Now, experience worketh hope."

IT was in Autumn that I first met Philip, and with Autumn, and all that belongs to it, he is forever associated to my mind; with walks through the rustling corn-fields, across the breezy, sunny hills; with rambles in the woods, the faint decaying odor of the fallen leaves, and the sound of our footsteps among them; with ripe nuts slipping from their husks; with the berry, the fir-apple, the acorn; with all that makes up Autumn's sober, exhilarating charm. And yet, more than with all of this, I connect him with that sense of rest and fulfilment, "the joy of harvest," which only Autumn brings. How bright, how confident was Philip! Yet his was a sober, I had almost said a *calculated* joy; it held by a firm root, being not so much a part of his nature as belonging to the whole of it. As we now stood together, I saw that I was not so much older than he as I had at first imagined; no, nor yet so much poorer; but his spoils had been won in the free sunlight, mine gathered from the darksome cave. What matter that they had been won hardly, even *snatched* from dark and slippery places, where my footing had wellnigh failed? what matter that they had now ceased to charm me? that I delight no longer in the dark glow of the carbuncle, in the opal's imprisoned fire? for thou, Philip, didst love and prize them, and they may serve thee for use and beauty when thy friend is here no longer.

Philip, too, had been, like me, a merchantman seeking goodly pearls. Beauty, knowledge, power, had each cast its deep spell over his spirit; his toils had been as severe as mine, yet mixed with far less of suffering, and this because he had ever been at home in the world. Growing as the tree, as the flower grows, from within, yet drinking freely, as they do, of air and dew and sunshine, for him, as regards each common, kindly outward influence, had that word been spoken, "Unto you are they given *for food.*" My life had been more restrained, less natural; it would sometimes seem to me that I formed no essential part of the things that surrounded me, that I even *lived* by effort and volition. Yet this secret sense of unfamiliarity sat heavily on my spirit; I had been like a stranger with a friendly heart, who, perplexed with the bustle of the family, smiles and tries to look as if he understands what it all means. Even when I had been most bewildered by the rush and clatter of the vast machinery of life, with its, to me, unintelligible wheels and springs, I had the most striven to knit myself up within the complicated web it wrought. I had sought to find for myself affinities which even in courting I had in some degree dreaded, for it was need rather than affection that drew me to them, and I knew not how dangerously powerful such alliances might prove; they returned my grasp closely, but was their pressure indeed kindly? Often I felt the steel gauntlet rather than the living hand. Might they not absorb the life they seemed to nourish? Yet while I had now wound myself round a sheltering elm, while I had now been driven to embrace the rock for a shelter, while I had been ever solicitous of some exterior help, some buttress that might support the fabric it seemed but to adorn, Philip's mind resting on a sure foundation, and tending to a fixed aim, had lifted up his whole life into the sunshine, self-poised, like the dome of Brunelleschi. His whole spiritual being was like a strongly-governed country, where all things fall, as it were, inevitably under a few fixed all-inclusive laws; the problems of life and thought perplexed, but did not overwhelm him; the enchanted forest of fancy was safe ground to one who held within his bosom the golden knife, ever ready to cut its clear, swift way, when the path became too entangled, the knot too hard.

Yet Philip was no special pleader even for Truth itself; he loved her for her own sake, too well to ask her "whence she came, or whither she was going"; he held her, I often thought, in a bold, loving clasp, as the maiden is held in the ancient legend: let her turn within his arms to sword or flame, let her change there into some fearful and monstrous shape, still would that fervent, unrelaxing grasp compel her to reveal herself in her true likeness; still within those very arms would she bless him. He knew that she would ofttimes make herself strange to him, and lead him through crooked paths; and where she led, he followed. He avoided no discussion; he shrank from no conclusion; yet it was interesting through all to watch his quiet, assured countenance, bright, I sometimes thought, with a sort of patient, anticipated triumph, like that of one to whom *the end* has been made surely known, though he has been left to find for himself the way. Duty, faith, accountability — all that the clear consciousness of spiritual freedom gives — were so strong in him as to determine the gravitation of his intellect, as well as that of his soul. To steadfast, implicit reliance on God, to simple, practical obedience to His law, he *must* come back after however strong and daring a flight. Therefore he, of all whom I have known, was best able to realize the evangelic privilege of serving the Lord *without fear.* Let him wander where he would, he could not get into a Far Country; the world was unto him the Father's house, and he the Son who was ever with him. His spirit was that of one to whom the day of life, from dawn to dusk, was emphatically the Day after which the Night cometh, wherein no man can work; and yet there was in him I know not what sweetness and candor of nature, that saved him from the narrowness that so often marks the compact, established mind. He was no slave of the Hours, to lie upon the grass and watch their flight, as it is marked by sun-gleam and shadow, by the opening and the closing flower. Yet each station of the day, each spot where the chariot of the sun rested, was dear to him: sunrise, evening, the broad golden noon, the bird's clear song, the sudden scent of bud and bough, the spring's overcoming rapture, — these might not tempt thee, Philip, to linger on thy way, yet which of them didst thou ever *miss?*

Often, it is true, I would accuse him, half

playfully, yet half seriously, of utilitarianism, in a wider field than that commonly assigned to it, yet utilitarianism still. "You love," I would say, "many things beautiful and excellent, not for their own sakes, but because they help and cheer you to a higher aim."

"And I," said Philip, "shall not be too careful to defend myself from that charge, or from the kindred one which you brought against me not many hours ago. When I listened so fixedly to your Scandinavian legend, I *was*, as you suspected, thinking of my Young Men's class, and of 'improving' it for their benefit when we meet this evening. But did this make me feel and enjoy its beauty less? I do not share Schiller's jealousy about making the Ideal useful; let her be so, when and as she pleases. She will not, it is true, toil or spin; she will not grind at the mill for any man; she will not be the wife of his bosom, his housemate and helpmeet, not even his steady, reliable friend. And yet does it not show how great Man's spirit is, that he should have needs to which none but this fair, proud

Queen can minister, weariness which she alone can soothe, griefs which only she can solace? There is a region within him in which she also *serves*, and serves no less truly because her action is, like that of all spiritual forces, irregular and intermittent, — an influence which comes unwooed, and departs unbidden, no more to be trained and disciplined than the lightning can be steadied into the fire of a household hearth, to live by and cook by. I have long loved art and poetry, because I saw that they had a power to raise and soften Humanity; more lately I have seen that *they are good in themselves*, — or whence, but from their native affinity with the things that are more excellent, should come this acknowledged power? Why, when the heart would reveal its truest, deepest instincts, does it seek to express itself in music? Why, when the mind would utter forth words of nobleness, — when it would be truer and sweeter than it can be under its ordinary conditions, does it speak in poetry? *Could* there be a prose psalm?"

"Even in dancing," I said, "there seems to

be something of this desire to escape into the region you speak of, *one less fettered*, but *more ordered* than that in which we ordinarily move. A subtle charm lies in the apparent freedom of the movement, and the sense of its being bound to the music; a pleasure akin to that which music itself gives us, in the knowledge that it must fall back upon an inevitable, rigorous law; its free, proud changes are like the movements of a queen in captivity. The mind loves to feel itself under a harmonious necessity,

> 'Breaking its order, yet still to that order returning,
> Changing and winding, yet true to its Measure and Law.'

And in obeying this it attains a double emancipation, for in confusion there is ever bondage; and it is to this confusion, the want of rhythm and cadence in life, the absence of a clear purpose and intention, that it owes so much of its weariness and sadness. Have you not felt how much there is in the ordinary inevitable course of life which genders to bondage? 'The strong hours conquer us.' We are straitened in ourselves and in each other, fettered to a routine which makes us often say, with John Bunyan, '*And so I went home to prison.*'"

"And this, as you say, is inevitable; we blame society for being constrained and artificial, but its conventionalities are only the result of the limitations of man's own nature. How much, for instance, of what is called 'reserve' belongs to this life, and passes away with its waning, and the waxing of the new life! We can say to the dying, and hear from them, things that, in the fulness of health and vigor, could not be imparted without violence to some inward instinct. And this is one reason, among many others, why it is so *good* to be in the house of mourning, the chamber of death. It is there more easy to be *natural*, — to be true, I mean, to that which is deepest within us. Is there not something in the daily, familiar course of life which seems in a strange way to veil its true aspect? It is not Death, but Life, which wraps us about with shroud and cerement. Looking at this world as it is, I could exclaim, How beautiful, *if one could but get at it!* I see in the heart of man an infinite desire, an infinite capacity for happiness; in the outward world, abundant materials for its satisfaction; but between these two, an unseen wall of separation. We want a door opening."

"The ordinary events of life," I said, "are not strong enough to move the whole man; its deeper and more passionate moments show us what we really are. There is a child within us that has not strength to come forth, until some outward stimulus, some strong exterior call, is given. And this, it seems to me, is the true use of the Heroic, of a life transcending life's ordinary possibilities; such a life is a direct call upon the soul, saying, 'Friend, come up higher'; and the heart recognizes its voice, and exults in it, *claims* it, as the voice of kindred risen to a more exalted sphere. It is like air from a mountain summit where we could not *live*, and yet it seems our native air, and braces us in every nerve."

"In teaching criminals," said Philip, "of a peculiarly ignorant and degraded class, I have often been struck with their strange susceptibility to what is morally exalted. To tell them of a deed of heroic daring, of sublime self-devotion, will visibly stir a fibre of their hearts, too torpid to respond to the ordinary appeals of duty and reason. I have also observed, that anything legendary, and verging on the supernatural, will fix their attention at once, as if it awakened within them the instinct of a spiritual nature, the sense that man lives not by bread alone. In teaching, perhaps, we usually trust too much to mere intelligence; surely there are many gateways into the soul. Feeling bursts through them, 'making the world kin.' Art unlocks them gently, for Art is not the imitation of Nature, but a sort of side-door into her inmost recesses. And has it never occurred to you to remark, that there is a whole region, connected with all that is finest and purest in our nature, that can only be reached through *sensation?* As a look will reveal what no word can ever speak, so will a scent, a sound, the spring's warm breath, the green unravelling of the larch-bough, a sudden whisper in the summer leaves, the bird's clear song at early morning, bring our souls into contact with the illimitable, telling us that we are one with ourselves, with Nature, and with God; these things have power to call forth a music within us which has not yet had words set to it. Secrets are revealed to us in a flash of bliss, — a flash that *shows* us nothing, as when a wave retires, and does not leave at our feet even a shell, which we can pick up, to treasure and say, 'This came from a further shore.'"

"But the sea," I said, "implies the shore; and it is something also to have heard the murmur of the broad ocean. I think that these moments, these intimations, which seem, as you once observed to me, to come from a great distance, prove many things, — prove, above all, that man's spirit is not a sand-locked pool. The slender filaments of sensation are threads that bind us to a mighty whole, and it is a higher, more complete existence, — *the life in the whole*, — which, through them, stirs in us, perhaps to sleep the next moment."

"Beethoven, if you remember," interrupted Philip, "said that music was the link between rational and sensitive life; it addresses both, and owes to this its power; for music, of all the arts, alone *reaches* to that within us, to which the others can only appeal. Like divine grace it gets fairly within the mind; and while things that address themselves to the eye or intellect stand at the door and knock, it has already carried in its message, and brought us into an inner world, richer and sweeter than the outward one, yet linked with it at every turn. What is there in life, *as it now is*, that answers to the feelings which music calls forth,—

> "Its deeper pangs, its tears
> More sweet,"—

its storming at the citadel of feeling through a hundred gates at once, or winning it through some single secret postern? You read, you think, you ponder, and, lo! a grinding organ at the corner of the street, playing some common tune, sends a fresh breath across your soul, that turns over a new leaf within it, writ all over with deeper, sweeter lore than was ever magician's book."

"And surely," I said, "in considering this

subject, we must not forget the strange regions into which some of the abnormal phases of mind admit us. What we commonly call "excitement," is but *the awakening of the whole man.* Is it not, whether it arise from some tumult of inner feeling, or the pressure of strong outward exigency, always accompanied by a feeling of freedom, of power over outward nature, of escape from the limitations of time and space, by a sense of being able to triumph over them at will? There is surely something significant in its temporary insensibility to cold, hunger, weariness; while excitement lasts, we feel none of these. Also, in dreaming, in delirium, or when under the influence of narcotics, the soul unfurls the wings, which life, under its ordinary conditions, keeps pressed and folded helplessly against its side. The sense of power, of freedom, above all, of *extension*, is characteristic of all these states; and does not this, as an admitted fact, throw a light upon our future life, *proving that man's capacities are as undeveloped as is confessedly the case with his faculties?* We are used to call the accustomed order of things natural, but is it not evident that man, viewed in connection with this order, is a supernatural being? He contains within him powers and tendencies far greater than the present order of things calls out."

"There is just now," said Philip, "a strange jealousy of the supernatural; a disposition, as shown in rejecting whatever is miraculous, to restrict even God to one mode of working. In moral things, it is true, he has, indeed can have, but one form of expression; but in material things, what is the supernatural but a stretching of the senses, so as to take in a little more of God, *an extension of our own horizon*, so as to give us a broader view of the way in which he acts? What is a miracle, once proved, but *a fact*, which extends our view of the capabilities of nature? How are we to limit the possibilities wrapped up within any created being, as the butterfly is anticipated, prepared for, in the grub, the oak latent in the acorn? Man, it is evident, even in that part of him which is sensitive, is forever touching upon a system of things upon which, under the present conditions of his being, he cannot enter fully. There is within him an enchanted land of mystery and beauty, a land where all slumbers, until some outward shock, like the kiss of the Fairy Prince, comes to awake it from sleep. So in that part of our nature which is spiritual, there is a region into which man cannot ascend until he is lifted there by God through that supernatural action upon the soul which we call *grace;* the voice of the Divine Spirit wakening up the human spirit to its true life."

"And hence," I said, "the connection of Christianity with poetry, music, nature, with all the purer and more exalted movements of the natural heart. These are helps, *lifts* to the soul; and people feel better, more able to believe, to love, to pray, when the finer springs of existence have been touched through any of these. Genius, like Christianity, sees all things in their mutual relation; its tendency is to throw the many-chambered mansions of the soul into one. The simplest song, where its breath is felt, stirs something which goes through the whole. Is there not a delight, almost a religious pleasure, in a work of true imaginative genius? a delight kindred to that which is derived from the contemplation of nature, — the delight of being carried out of one's self into something greater and *truer* than self, because more universal. It often seems to me that Imagination is the highest faculty of man. It starts, as Faith does, from a higher level than any of his other powers, and on that level meets and familiarly accosts truths which reason must struggle up to. And reason *does* reach them, when they are thus foreshown, though, left to itself, it could never either have foreseen the glorious end, nor even the way that led to it."

"Imagination, however," returned Philip, "'wins heights that it is not competent to keep'; it alights on the mountain-top, and is shown kingdoms in a moment of time; but it cannot keep its footing on that summit. Reason must hew steps out of the rock; patient experience must follow after to make the path in which the wayfaring man shall not err."

"And yet," I said, "the Idealist is always

the discoverer, the one who proclaims the goodly vision. It has ever been so in science; there is something prophetic in its very nature, something which ever impels it forward, and carries it beyond the word it is now speaking; which *weights* that word with a meaning which the speaker intends not. So does the Poet speak out of his heart things which he knows not. He is a man not truer, better, or kinder than his fellows; his range of practical sympathies with others is, perhaps, from his very nature, more limited than that of ordinary men. It is not experience, it is not feeling, it is instinct, that has made him at home in all that belongs to man. He sits beside the secret springs of feeling, and knows the course the rivers must take. He sees, but afar off and dimly, the whole in which the part is included. *He who has the soul has all.*"

Philip's eyes sparkled. "I know," he said, "no such pleasure, such emancipation, as that of passing from the limited self-referring view of things into the contemplation of absolute truth and beauty. I love to hear you speak thus, you, who sometimes seem to fear the broad, free sweep of imaginative greatness, as being in some way antagonistic to the spirit of Christ, who seem to dread, for instance, the free development of Art, though, after all, Art is but Nature in her bridal hour, the shy virgin, the wild woodland nymph wooed and wedded by man, and brought home to dwell with him."

"I know not," I said, "how to express clearly what I mean; but I do feel, sometimes painfully, a contradiction between the brokenness of Christ and the clear perfection of Art. The glory of the Terrestrial is one, and the glory of the Celestial is another, and these stars differ, the one from the other in glory. In Art there is choice, self-pleasing, a drawing out of that which is obviously best; in Christ, things which are not fair are yet pronounced good, prizeable. Sometimes, after reading such a book, we will say, as Shakespeare, I have been conscious of a strange inner dissatisfaction, which I can only describe as being the sense of an impaired communion; and something has said within me, 'All this is not of the Father, but of the world.'

I do not feel this in reading any book of a sustained philosophic interest, as its scope, if not directly religious, carries you among the deep and elevating realities which are not far from the Kingdom, and indeed belong to it; but I do feel it in that mixed region of wit, and fancy, and feeling which belongs to our mortal state *as such*, and which seems in no way to bear upon our inner or our future life; and what is this region but a world without souls, a world of sad and ruined beauty, when looked at with reference to man's true destinies, and yet a rich and glorious world? I see in Art and Literature, in the subjects with which they deal, in the absorbing, intoxicating devotion they demand, something which reminds me of the Greek worship of Dionysus, "the God of flourishing, decaying, changeable life," the kindler of a lofty enthusiasm, *the intensifier of life*, the exalter of its pleasures, the deepener of its pangs, the bestower of an impassioned sympathy with Nature. And by the side of this regal Being, robed in the purple he was born to, with garments not too careful of a stain, I see another form, severe, restricted, also life's deepener, its intensifier, but after how different a spirit! The first is of the earth, earthy; the second is the Lord from heaven.

> "The rose, ho! the rose is the grace of the earth,
> Is the light of the plants that are growing upon it."

The rose drunk with its own fragrance and beauty; the smell of the fresh earth hangs about it, — it is wet with the dews of heaven. 'Enjoy me,' it says, 'for I am the rose, I am fair, I live but a day'; it needs the broad sunlight, the free sweeping winds, it can bloom even on the battle-field, and grow redder with the blood of heroes. But Christ's flower grows underneath the snow, in a broken flower-pot, in a darkened cellar, anywhere; its petals are pale, and it seldom opens fully; but when it expands so as to show its heart, what do we see there but the Cross and the emblems of the Passion?" . . . .

Philip was silent a long while; at last he said, musingly, —

"I have felt the antagonism you speak of. I have found it out, as I have found out many antagonisms and affinities, by their helping or hindering me in my work. I shall never forget sitting at an open window of a little parsonage, in the west of England, during great part of a golden summer's afternoon, reading Keats; the garden was full of flowers, and I read my book to the scent of mignonette and pinks, as to a music stealing within every sense. It was one of those warm, brooding days that steep the spirit in delight; all around was silence, the stillness not so much of sleep as of nature in a blissful dream. Then an uneasy consciousness came across me, breaking the delicious spell. I ought to be setting forth on my parish round. I started. First on my list came an aged woman, almost stone-deaf, ignorant, but anxious. I had to sit beside her before a huge fire; her son worked at his loom in an inner room, and did not cease when I began to read. How hot and noisy the cottage seemed; how contracted all around me! Had the world of light and beauty I lived and moved in but half an hour ago *collapsed* into this? How confused, too, seemed my own statements, my very utterance thick and hesitating, as of one under a heavy thrall, for my heart was with Endymion, and I had to tell the story of Christ; to tell it from its beginning to its end; to tell it, too, to a person to whom it was really *news*, and received as such with eager childlike interest. . . . . Another time, and here the revulsion was even keener, this was in winter, New Year's day, also an afternoon; one of those days when the clear frosty air seems to make thought itself more definite, and to send it forth with an arrowy keenness. You know the cathedral at ——; I was walking beneath it with a friend, eagerly discussing Homer; the sun went down, all that fine range of buildings stood up clear against the solemn, rose-flushed sky. We spoke of the antique world; its simplicity, its freedom, its ever youthful, self-renewing charm. I was suddenly called away to see a woman supposed to be dying. I found her, as regarded spiritual receptivity, far below the old friend I have just spoken of. Hers was the unawakened, unenlightened mind, within which the sense of sin and need has never sent a piercing ray, or a quickening throb; one of the class to whom a visit from a clergyman is a viaticum and nothing more. Her husband, an elderly working-man, received me at the door with much show of friendliness; as he seemed disposed to talk, I sat with him a few minutes before I went to the sick woman. By way, I suppose, of making himself agreeable to me, he brought forth some tracts, and began to speak of religion in a patronizing sort of way, not uncommon amongst the poor, as if it were an accomplishment, something admirable in its own way,—an acquisition, like knowing French or Latin, to those who possessed it, but by no means of universal obligation. 'Yes,' he said, 'they were very pretty reading, he had no fault to find with them; prayer, too, was a nice thing; good talk was very pretty and very nice.' I found that neither he nor any of his family ever attended church, or any place of worship. He took me to a small inner room, dark and close, in which were two beds, almost filling it. The sick woman was in one, suffering much from spasms, too ill apparently to fix her mind upon what I said. I spoke with her, however, as I best could. Seating myself, in the absence of any chair, upon the other bed, suddenly I felt something move beneath me. The poor woman hastened to apologize: it was her grown-up son sleeping off the drunken frolic of the night before, — New Year's Eve."

"But these," I said, laughing, "were very sharp contrasts, very sudden descents into the actual; no wonder your system was jarred and shaken a little rudely. You might have been called to such a dying-bed as that you were telling me of yesterday, the poor woman, "the sinner exceedingly," who had spent literally more than half of her short and evil life in prisons, dying in jail at last, ignorant, hopeless, yet not without hope, for Christ died for the ungodly. In such a case the transition from the ideal to the actual would have been keen, perhaps, but less perplexing."

"True," returned Philip, "because in the human soul 'one deep calleth to another.' There is a poetry in crime, in excessive want and wretchedness, in fact in all the fierce extremes of life, that lifts the soul above its ordinary level, that stirs human nature to its very depths, and makes us know that

> 'We have all of us one human heart,
> All mortal thoughts confess a common home.'

Life can be transfigured through anguish as well as through blessedness, and Christ still shows himself, as in the mediæval legends, in the form of the leper and the outcast. But after all, such keen emotions do not make up the staple of spiritual any more than of natural life. It is among the ignorant, the out-of-the-way, the *commonplace*, that the Christian's daily lot is thrown, and their daily appeals are to him as sacred as those which come more seldom, and with a louder knocking at the gate. That Christianity should so fit in with the ordinary and mediocre has always seemed to me a proof of its crowning excellence. 'A little child shall lead them,' this, it seems to me, is the pass-word into this kingdom of greatness and simplicity. All other ideals draw away the heart from real life; the poet, the artist, is continually trying to break out of the narrow circle of visible things; he 'asks for better bread than can be made with wheat.' The Christian ideal alone meets the habitual, the practical, — *meets it while immeasurably transcending it*, — embraces it, and walks with it hand in hand. The Christian must be friends with every day, with its narrow details, its homely atmosphere; its loving correction must make him great."

He paused for a moment.

"Is there not," he said, "the very life-core of Christianity in this picture, — the broken tomb and the risen Christ, the angels in their shining garments, the linen clothes *folded*, and laid in a place by themselves?"

ONE morning I found Philip looking over some of my papers; he took up one, "A Soul's History," and began to read it aloud.

"The soul is a rare essence; like the quick
And subtle spirit of the rose, it floods
Each chamber of its earthly house with fragrance,
Yet leaves, like it, no lingering breath behind,
Its sweetness taking with it where it goes;
Else had this grave, like His, who, once of old,
Slept in a garden-tomb, been full of odors;
And through this bare, black ground would roses spring,
To tell of one who lies within, wrapt round
In folds of linen clean and white; embalmed
In sweeter tears than ever fell from gums
Of Araby the Blest.

"Beside this open grave one winter morn
I stood as if alone, the hundreds round me
Swayed by one thought, and by a single name

Together bound so close, it seemed one heart
Held by one sorrow, by one hope uplifted;
Upon the stillness fell the words of Christ:
'I am the life, and I the resurrection;
He that in me believeth shall not die';
And through the sound of falling earth, the voice
Went steadfast on: 'As God unto himself
In mercy hath been pleased to take the soul
Of this our *Brother*'—pausing ere the word
It faltered forth—'of this our *Father*'; then
One sob broke forth, for, oh! on this our earth
We have not many Fathers! few who go
To meet the wanderer on his homeward way,
Who watch him yet afar, who on the threshold
With welcome wait, and reconciling tear.

"Thou knewest him, this man of faith and power;
Thou knewest him, this Son of Consolation,
God's Levite of the kindlier covenant.
On thine his soul, a white and lucid star,
Shook down serene its full meridian splendor,
For thou didst know him in that after-summer
God ofttimes gives the good, that they may see
Their soul's deep travail satisfied in part,
And bless him ere they pass from life away;
But I had known him in his rise and falling,
Had seen him sit upon the earth, as one
Astonished, desolate, within his heart
An arrow and the fragments of a song.

"'*What aileth thee that now*
Thou comest back so soon, my child;

In that garden fair, methought, all day,
Till the shadows fell thou wouldst wait to play" ;
So spake the mother mild.

" But the child said, weeping sore,
' I have been where the roses blow,
The ruby red and the maiden's blush,
And the damask rose in its velvet flush,
And the white rose dropping snow.

" ' I will never pluck roses more,
Go take of these. . . .' "

" I like this poem," he said. " Why have you left it unfinished ? "

I looked at the date, which was many years back. " Perhaps," I answered, " because my heart, since those days, has, in some degree, departed from the idea upon which it is founded."

" And your idea," said Philip, " was that of a life rising, through earthly blight and disappointment, into high spiritual perfection ; the flowers of individual love dropping off to give place to ripe, universal charity. I see you have written, a little further on, —

' *Seek not to live, to die in any heart.*
This earthly rose, if pressed, will yield the thorn;
O, let it bloom, its odor still diffusing ! ' "

"Yes," I said, "the idea of a beautiful moral and spiritual life, being built up out of the ruins of the fair fabric of natural hope and happiness, is a favorite one, we all know, in religious fiction; take, as an instance, Lamartine's exquisite story of the Stone-cutter of St. Point; and it has undoubtedly been in some degree realized in actual life, but far less often and less fully than the commonplaces which prevail with reference to affliction would lead us to believe. All that passes current upon this subject is founded upon a partial truth, which ignores a deeper one, which is this, that the plant of Humanity does not live by its root only, however firmly this may be fixed; it breathes at every pore, through leaf and blossom; it is nourished by the curling tendrils that seem but to adorn it. If these be torn off too unsparingly, its fruit will be the poorer; if its bark be stripped, it will live, but as dying. How often do we see the growth of a life stopped! — a life unable, either from the blight of unfriendly outward circumstances, or the strange warp of some radical inward contradiction, to reveal the true beauty of its nature."

"It seems to me," said Philip, "that I have known such lives, unable to shoot up straight to heaven, like the palm, or to bend down richly laden to earth, like the banian; lives off the usual track; lives in which there is a painful secret, and yet pure, exalted lives; truer and nobler in their aim, richer even in their attainment, than those whose development has been more free and happy; souls that utter not their perfect worth, yet are sweet in the very brokenness of their music."

"True; yet it is certain that something artificial and distorted is apt to creep within a life, which, from whatever cause, is unable to flow along in the broad channel of such interests as are common to humanity. There are many ghosts in life, appearing in the noonday as well as at midnight. Dead hopes and loves come back in strange forms; tenderness changed to an irritable sensitiveness; clinging affection to grasping vanity. The tendrils that have lost their natural object still find something to cling round; but what? A cold ambition; a thin transfiguration of self. Do you know the story of Agusina, the Greenlander, one of the most earnest and gifted among the converts of the United Brethren? His own people would listen to him with singular veneration, as he spoke to them of Christ, of the breath of the Spirit, 'wafting the heart to Him, as the sea-grass is driven to shore on the current of the tide.' 'His love,' he would say, 'melts the heart, as the sun melts the snow; and then it is as with the lamp, when fresh oil is poured into it; it burns brighter, and can enkindle others. O Assarsoi!* when I speak of thee, my heart grows tender, as the moss in spring, and soft, as the eider fowl's breast, when sheltering its young!' He had an only daughter, Beata, aged fifteen, who read the Scriptures to him each evening, when their voices were heard to ascend together in hymns. His wife was dead; all his near relations, parents, brother, and sisters, were gone, but not until he had persuaded them to embrace Christianity. Beata prepared his meals, and took charge of all; when he came home from his hunting or fish-

* Redeemer.

ing, she would stand anxiously waiting his return. She, too, was taken from him by death. Agusina bore the shock but feebly. Except Christ, he said, she was his all on earth; he missed his loved companion, when he came from the sea or from the mountains; even the words of Scripture, heard from her lips no longer, seemed to lose half their charm. He gave way to excessive sorrow; but it was after the first violence of this passed over, that the missionaries observed a singular transformation. Self-complacency rushed in to fill the void which had fallen on his desolated soul; his heart became self-centred; it found a solace in the respect paid by his people; a flattering unction in the veneration and interest with which, at the gatherings for hunting and fishing, they listened to his words. There was a change even in his outward aspect and bearing, a change visible to all. At last one of the faithful Moravians spoke to him of it freely; he listened in surprise and displeasure. A few days afterwards, however, he came, confessing it was true; that he had striven to deal with himself faithfully, and that God had given him light: his mind was still so disturbed that he absented himself from the Holy Communion. And weeks passed over; no one saw Agusina at the meetings or the confessions; and when the Moravians sought him out, they found him, they say, 'in happy intercourse with the Friend of his soul, but with the hand of death upon him.' He was going, he said, to Beata; 'earth was no longer safe for him; it was full of snares; and God was, in his mercy, about to take him away.' On the last day of his life, his people gathered round him. All the strength and self-possession of his soul had returned. 'His countenance,' says the Moravian writer, 'seemed to us like that of an angel.' In the dim December day, more by the light of the snow than of the sky, they laid him, with a solemn prayer and hymn, in his Beata's grave, close to her moss-wrapped remains.

"This story has always seemed to me deeply affecting, and the more so from my having, not many years ago, heard a pendant to it, in the case of a distinguished man now living, in whose character vanity of a transparent sort had always been noticeable; yet it was remarkable, I was told, into what strong, unsubdued relief this had come since the death of his beloved *only* child. But, to consider this subject in a broader light, — is there not something fallacious in looking at affliction as a sort of divine alchemy, with power *in itself* to transmute and sublimate? At the most, it can but work upon what it finds; it purges the dross from the gold, according to the image so frequently employed in Scripture, but does not change the original nature of the ore into one of nobler quality.

"And to extend our view a little further, can anything be more false than the so often repeated maxim, that good comes out of evil, moral evil? — *never*, in the sense of being produced by it. All that evil can do, is to make good manifest; as oppression calls forth heroism, or, as in family life, the selfishness of one member brings out the excellence of another. Yet, in the very instances where this is most admirably shown, we may still say, that 'if one member suffer, all the members suffer with it'; all life is organic, and no individual ever neglects or violates a moral or social obligation, but a wound, more or less directly felt, goes through the whole. The work of righteousness is peace; the natural tendency of good is to reproduce itself: even so does evil sow itself *ad infinitum;* unless, through repentance, it ceases to be evil, and even, after repentance, the seed beforehand cast into the earth *will still come up.* We see this in the life of nations. What confusion and anarchy result from forced appropriation and unequal laws! A life may slowly get over a great sorrow, but when does a country get over a great wrong? Germany was at least two centuries in recovering from the effects of the Thirty Years' War, and it is certain that Italy yet suffers from the desolating invasions of the sixteenth century. What has Ireland been to England, or Poland to Russia, but a standing perplexity from age to age? What else is the African population even now to America? *It is not only the wronged who suffer.* The roots of Humanity are so inextricably intertwined, that we must grow altogether if we grow at all. Every warp and canker tells upon the whole."

"True," said Philip, "as regards evil of a moral kind; but in pain and affliction, into which this element does not enter, I see much of the alchemy which you disallow. There is something in man which *needs* sorrow, a humbling, purifying work as regards his spiritual recreation, which cannot go on without its ministry. How many heavenly seeds would never spring to life but for its loosening, detaching agency, breaking up the hard, stony soil of nature! And to the believer, what is affliction but God's hand upon his head to bless him, his Father's hand, *recognized* through that heavy pressure? Think how Christianity exalts, almost enthrones sorrow."

"Because," I said, "Christianity itself is among us as one that is wounded, 'free among the dead,' and only free there. Do you not see that Christianity, under its present manifestation, is *remedial*, separation and sorrow are its natural friends? Consider, for instance, how great, even to disproportion, is the strain which the Gospel lays upon the passive qualities of the soul, *those which tend to the death of the natural man*,—acquiescence, long-suffering, self-abnegation. The Earth is given to the meek, and Heaven to the poor in spirit. Christ's kingdom is a kingdom of patience. Think of that solemn walk, when he 'went before' his disciples to Jerusalem; his counsel of absolute self-renunciation to the young ruler; his acceptance of Peter's 'Lo! we have left all'; his rebuke to the self-seeking of the two brethren; his unfolding of his own approaching humiliation. What is it but a call to Humanity to strip off its garments one by one, riches, affection, glory, and lay them down in the way by which its Lord walks to death."

"If I follow your meaning clearly," returned Philip, "you would say that there is a natural grandeur and completeness, which the soul, if it would have Christ formed within it, must be content to miss."

"And this because Christianity does not *as yet* take in the whole of man; it is the bringer of the sword, setting one part of his nature in array against the other; it bids him emphatically lay down his life, but to what end? *That he may take it again.* We do not gain a true conception of Christianity until we look at it under this twofold aspect; until we see in it a seed sown in weakness to be raised in power; until we covet, for every individual soul, that restitution which the Universal Church will one day most certainly enjoy, — the taking again of life in Christ. Christ is most truly and deeply a man of sorrows; yet in his revelation there is nothing of that dull and aimless suffering which in natural life is so saddening and perplexing. The song of Moses and of the Lamb, which none but the redeemed can sing, has the burden of the old Greek chorus,

> 'Sing sorrow, strife and sorrow, but let Victory remain!'

Understand well that I do not disallow sorrow; it has its appointed time and work, but when that is over, let it go; it is a hireling, and remaineth not in the house forever; but the son remaineth ever, — and the son is Isaac, a son of laughter. Nothing appears to me more shallow, than the mode of viewing life which looks upon pain 'as the deepest thing in our nature, and union through pain the closest of any.' Sorrow is essentially separative. What is its extremest form — insanity — but isolation? The French, with as much truth as tenderness, call the insane *les aliénés*. The mind, broken in itself, has lost the power of blending with other minds; its action returns upon itself. Joy is a uniting thing; it builds up, while it enlarges, the whole nature; it is the wine to strengthen man's heart, to brace it to every noble enterprise. Schiller's crown was well won with that one saying, '*Was ist dem Glücklichen zu schwer?*'"

"'*Res severa est verum gaudium*,'" said Philip. "I have sometimes thought, that, as regards spiritual things, we shall not arrive at this, the bringing in of the sacrifices of joy, except through a fuller realization of our organic unity in Christ. Gladness can scarcely be a solitary thing, the very life of praise seems choral, it is more than one bounded heart can utter. Its finest expressions are those that, in the Psalms, and some ancient Canticles, call on Nature, even that which is not conscious and animate, to swell its harmony: —

> 'O ye showers and dew, praise ye the Lord!'

Once, even in music, I was content with melody; a *tune*, with its sweetness, like that of a tinkling rill, was enough to gladden me; now my heart asks for a deeper spell. Surely when one has once entered into the blissful secrets of harmony, the note seems to suggest the chord, to *ask* to be built up within it."

"What you say reminds me of a strange pleasure, the intense consciousness of existence, which one sometimes feels in a crowd, especially if that crowd be animated by one common feeling, and that of an exalting kind. Life seems lifted out of its ordinary conditions, as if in the whole it recovered something which the part had missed. Does the heart in these moments reclaim some wide affinity, and ask to be built within the human chord?"

"I think," said Philip, "there is some feeling akin to this in the pleasure which *exten-*

4

sion gives, something which intensifies feeling, through bringing within it the sense of infinity, as when we gaze over any great reach of country, with the cattle upon a thousand hills, or across the sea, with ships dropping under the rim of the horizon. In the sight of any great town from some little distance, or in looking down at evening upon some sheltered hamlet, what a deep and tender sentiment steals across the mind! We know that the city is not the Celestial one, neither is the village Arcadian, yet the impression left upon the heart is one of peace, 'Peace and good-will with all mankind.' Breadth always imparts the feeling of serenity; all that is narrow and contradictory melts away in it.

> 'Colors laid
> Upon the canvas oft the sense invade
> Too suddenly, and wound the aching eye;
> *Yet when did aught beneath the open sky*
> *Seem harsh or violent?* So sun and shade
> Attemper all.'

Even so in contemplating men, say soldiers, weavers, colliers, in a collective body, we feel the heart drawn out in a deeper sympathy and interest, which none among them, perhaps, as individuals, would command. I have felt this strongly without being able to analyze it."

"Does it not arise from being brought within the influence of the broad tendencies of humanity, where individual limitations disappear, swept away by the force of the current? Such moments say to us, 'Behold the Man!'—they are baptismal, and endue the soul with much strength. The slender stream of individual life is choked by many rocks and rapids; the strongest heart knows that there are stones upon which it has already fallen and been broken, that barriers are before it never to be wholly overpast; therefore it loves to hope, to *strive* for the many. Passion, interest, caprice, belong to the individual, and in this, surely, lies the strength of the saying, *Vox populi, vox Dei*, that a number of persons acting together are naturally less under the control of circumstance, 'this world's unspiritual God,' are less fettered by prejudice, than the few. Also we know that in every lump there is a leaven of nobleness, some, perhaps many, tender and truthful souls. The heart of a people, if it could but speak, *is always in its right place.*"

"And it is this," said Philip, "that makes all that belongs to national existence, the songs, the customs upon which the life of a people has left its stamp, so interesting, so unspeakably affecting."

"And it is this, too," I continued, "which gives such a double dye to all sins against national freedom, which is but the expression of a people's life. If it is a crime to slay a man, what must it be to strike at a nation; *to kill man in his organic life;* to cut the nerves of universal endeavor; to aim at man's heart through those relations with his fellow-men, which are the veins through which his life-blood flows, in which alone he can live and move and have his secular being? *Slavery stabs man both in his individual and in his organic life,* and every minor degree of oppression is the snapping of a bond which knits one man to his fellows, and the whole man to God. The oppressed man does not *live.* There are no crimes so great as political crimes. To break faith with a nation is to break a deeper trust, to blight a fuller hope, than can be involved in any treachery towards an individual. Who is this, the true Antichrist, he that denieth the Father and the Son, but the absolutist, the tyrant? We are not surely sufficiently sensible of the Atheism involved in the deep iniquity of oppression. *It is the denial of God, through the denial of man;* the setting up of what is partial and arbitrary against that which is universal; in other words, *the assertion of will against law.*"

"The Lord is the Spirit, and where the Spirit of the Lord is *there* is liberty, because there only is the recognition of man's spiritual prerogative, the freedom of the will, the power to choose. All rational legislation is founded upon the idea of man's being a *governable* being, and this, in its turn, rests upon the basis of a moral and intelligent Governor of the world. When a community has lost faith in God, it cannot achieve freedom for man, even when it starts, as in the French Revolution, with being fanatically in love with it; it quickly relapses into absolutism, and the governing of the masses by force.

All materialism genders to bondage ; it is linked with the ideas of fate and necessity; they are its *powers*, and they leave room for but one worship, *that of the God of Forces.* How strange it seems that the idea of liberty should ever be associated with that of lawlessness, when, in fact, it is the arbitrary, which is really unsettled and reversible, depending on the breath which called it forth. All national greatness requires that which can only coexist with freedom, a slow, safe growth under assured protection; *law not depending on power, but power being founded upon law.*"

. . . . .

"And how much," resumed Philip, "is the spirit of Freedom connected with the sentiment of nationality! A slave has no country, no national existence, and wherever there is a strong awakening to liberty, it does not find expression, as might have been looked for, in a broad cosmopolitanism, but in bringing out more fully the distinctive physiognomy of each people. When a nation grows, it grows as an individual does, in its own shape. I sometimes wonder how far this tendency will act upon the future destinies of the great Church of Christ. There is nothing more evident in the whole history of the Church of Rome, than its hostility to all development of a national kind, its determination to mould, at whatever cost, the European world to its own pattern."

"Will it any longer," I said, "receive that pattern?"

"I know not; but Rome's hand, ever firm linked with that of material despotism, cannot now, in the nature of things, lie so heavy on the nations, as in the days when these two gave their power and strength to each other. Will the breaking up of Popery be connected with the rise of churches really national, able to *feed* the flocks of which they are the guardians; churches built upon the rock of Christ, in all that concerns faith and doctrine, yet, because Christ lives, *living* also, advancing with the advancing age, able to understand its needs, to interpret its aspirations, to give it back those very aspirations, clothed as Aaron was, in garments of glory and of beauty,—churches whose priests, like those of old, will 'go before' the people? It seems to me that the Church of Scotland, if not such a Church as this, is at least a national Church, fitting the national character, so that it is hard to say whether it was made for the Scotch, or they for it; it is the educator and guide of the people, the *expression* of their intellectual and spiritual life, the home of the poor man's affections and hopes. Such also, I believe, but here I cannot speak from personal observation, is Roman Catholicism in Ireland; a guide, a companion, a familiar friend, that to which the national heart turns. In England the Established Church has missed this; it has not won the heart of the poor."

"And yet," I said, "the Church of England also *represents* England, and perhaps in that aspect of it, which falls short of what exalted minds desire, it illustrates a very valuable part of the national character. The tendency of the English mind is practical, it is not remorseless in its logical requirements; it is content to leave many things as it finds them, undetermined, to work with them as they are. The English mind has never shown itself in love with an ideal; in political things it has never drawn forth the image of liberty, in clear abstract perfection, as the French have done. Freedom does not sit for her picture in England. Why should she, when we have her going in and out among us, a daily household friend, whose features are too familiar to be much noticed? So in the things of God, the English mind is one that must have room. It sees that the Bible is not a systematic book, neither is the Church a symmetrical building, nor the exigencies of the human spirit of the kind that can be sounded by line, or mapped out by compass, and it does not insist upon making them what they are not."

"In individuals," said Philip, "I can see how the very desire for completeness springs from a limited view of life, from failing to see how great, complicated, and out-reaching a thing it is. To minds of this class all truth appears under a strict and absolute aspect, to which life as it is cannot respond; this, joined to a pure and rigid conscientiousness, gives you the man who, like Lamennais, breaks not only the whole purpose of his life, but his heart itself, over his fair, unfound ideal. Among all nations, the English, as you say, have least of this, and of that which goes along with it, a tendency to fanaticism, where the mind is so driven up to a single truth, as to seek to explain all nature by it, wrenching, lopping off whatever does not, will not, *fit*. But, on the other hand, we miss in some degree what the more ardent, if more limited, nature arrives at, — that which makes martyrs, missionaries."

"And yet," I said, "even here we have not been found wanting, and shall not be. There is a practical enthusiasm, and this is ours; an energy which will not kindle up for an abstract truth, but which, once convinced of the motive excellence of such, once finding it work towards a tangible, worthy aim, will carry it out with unflinching perseverance. All that the English nation needs is to believe more implicity than it has yet done, and then it will work wonders. It is now high noon with us; what we, with the universal Church, need, is the midday miracle, the Light, like that which appeared unto Saul of Tarsus, above the brightness of the sun, in the clear conviction of the understanding, the full consent of the will, the turning of the heart to God, whose Word endureth forever in heaven. *When we believe in miracles, when we expect them, then we shall see them, then we shall work them, and not until then.*"

"Some years ago," said Philip, "I read some interesting tracts on Church subjects by a Mr. Applegarth, in which he remarked that there had always been a lurking Pelagianism in the Church of England. I did not understand at the time what he meant; but since then I have seemed to discover this tendency, in its remarkable deadness to the gifts and calling of the Holy Spirit. Any drawing to a closer and more devoted walk with Christ is apt to be set down to the score of enthusiasm, and is not recognized, as I think it is in almost every other communion, as coming from God. Witness the pertinacious attachment of Presbyterianism to its 'called' ministry, the 'leadings' of Quakers and Moravians, the 'vocation' of the Church of Rome.

There is a timidity and half-heartedness about us in this matter, which is unworthy of what we are in others; a want of clearly recognizing the consequences of those great spiritual facts which we speculatively accept as true.

"And I think the same timidity and want of confidence in a Divine leading is shown in our superstitious dread of discussion and alteration. A people that believes the Bible to be from God will not fear to appeal often and searchingly to human reason; a Church that believes in the Trinity will not be very jealous to retain the Athanasian Creed. In true faith there is nothing of a vice-like, mechanical grasp; its hold is firm and free; because it holds with the living hand, it can afford to let go what it no longer needs, while Formalism is like the false mother in Solomon's judgment, it cares not whether the child be alive or dead, so long as it is *there*, to be shown when it is asked for. It seems admitted now on all hands, that our Church would gain much by adaptation and elasticity; shorter and more varied services, a fuller recognition of the services of the laity, would do much to endear her to the people. Yet we run on in the accustomed groove. The most difficult chapters from the Old Testament are constantly read in our churches; but when the sermon comes, it contains no word of comment, of explanation; it makes no attempt to throw light upon those yet more difficult passages of human experience, to which our hearts, our homes, every hour bear witness, and which it is the glory of the Gospel to reconcile: it is generally the Gospel *unapplied.* The views which are presented to us are true, but brought into no relation with what we are doing or thinking about. God's commands are as little arbitrary as they are grievous; there is in the two Sacraments, in Prayer, in all things ordained by Him, *a rationale:* why not sometimes present us with it?"

"One thing," returned Philip, "is abundantly significant of our present time; it will not, as former ages have done, rest under the shadow of forms and creeds in which it does not believe. In reading the history of those times, you must have been struck with the real, yet wholly unvivifying belief, which people of the most evil hearts and lives kept upon the great central truths of revelation, and this in the case of both Catholics and Protestants. A trebly-dyed murderer, like Leicester, commends himself in his will 'to the alone merits of Jesus Christ,' with a fervor which is not quite hypocrisy, but something which is, I think, even more fearful. Nothing is to me more strange and appalling than their general acceptance of these truths as mathematical certainties, as things laid alongside of their actual life, without ever touching or quickening their spiritual consciousness. I have seen something of this in a less repulsive form among the poor of our own age, — belief and conscience running on in two parallel lines which never meet; also, among people of the last generation, a belief in revelation, and a respect for it, which is not vivifying, and yet is belief, if not faith. But *we* do not, cannot, so accept these eternal verities. Our age needs more, asks more. Its Church must be a sheltering tree, stretching out her boughs unto the river, and her branches unto the sea; not a pyramid, however awful and venerable, that does but cast a shadow across the desert. How significant are the notices, that now reach us, from those who are familiar with the signs of spiritual life on the Continent! Materialism making rapid strides, both in Protestant and Romish countries; persons of the class who would formerly have lived under the forms of religion, without being influenced by its power, are now rejecting it as a whole, professing open disbelief in all save that which can be seen and experienced; denying the capability of man to know anything of the unseen world. And yet, alongside of this, in Protestant and Romish countries alike, is growing up a counter movement; sometimes shown, as in part of the Lutheran Church, in a return and a passionate attachment to the old forms and creeds, which are now to it things having and giving life; sometimes appearing under less-defined outlines; a soul, perhaps, that still wants a body to work in; a desire of the heart towards Christ and his appearing. There is at present a sifting of the nations, and when it is over, this that cannot be shaken will remain. It sometimes seems to me that we are on the verge of a great constructive era. Men are beginning to repair the old wastes, the desolations of many generations. The Critical is now having its day; we may compare its work to that clearing away, which is the first sign of improvement; but its day must pass, as nothing of a simply negative kind can be lasting. Then comes a glad rebuilding, of which I can but prophesy dimly; but I foresee that the person and work of Christ will be its centre.

"And 'He, when he is lifted up, will draw all men unto him.' Is there not among us a manifest desire for union, an impatience of those Shibboleths, those inner tests, which, in Protestant countries, tend to needless exclusivism and separation; an impatience with all that, like the arrogant pretensions of Rome, making itself alone in the earth, renders equal communion and reciprocal interchange impossible? Is there not now among us a core of vital religion, a hidden Church waiting as a fruit-tree in spring will wait long, all set with blossom, for a day warm enough to blow in, *a day when it will blow all at once?*"

SOMETIMES," said Philip, "calling many tendencies of our age to mind, I wonder whether, as regards spiritual science, our future may not be more synthetical than any past age has been; will there not be less of analysis, of separation, — a greater disposition to look at things in their mutual relation? The study of natural science is ever tending to form this habit of mind within us."

"So much so," I said, "that even in art we can scarcely now be satisfied with that which does not, at least by implication, present us with something of the whole. Whatever is painted lovingly, whether broadly or minutely, does this. David Cox flings you down a page of nature in writing, scarcely legible from emotion; rough, blurred lines bring before you the wet reaches of sand, the ever-widening moor, the darkening sky, the wind blowing where it listeth, and make you feel as if you were among them, bound within the wings of sadness, beauty, and mystery, and carried you know not whither. So will one of W. Hunt's moss-grown, leafy, primrose-studded hedge-banks give you the breath and bloom of spring, the sense of the woods and fields, and of the broad open sky, within the compass of a few square inches. But there is a way of depicting nature and life, which, because we feel that it is not true to the whole, satisfies the understanding as little as it delights the heart; it takes feature by feature, and yet the picture is not like, because the expression — *that which belongs to the whole, and cannot be had without it* — is not there. Thackeray, for instance, takes up some fair and cherished ideal of humanity, pulls it in pieces, and says, 'You thought this was a lovely, breathing form; you loved it, mourned over it, but see, it is a doll; it never lived, its eyes are glass, I can show you the wires by which they open and shut. This withered flower that you have kept within your heart's book so long, that its leaves still open at the place where it is pressed, is *not* a flower; it never drank in the dew, or spread its leaves in the sunshine. Your treasure is a thing of shreds and patches, held together by a little gum.' Yet life is still beautiful and beloved. Love and truth and constancy, all things the human heart believes in, *remain;* and that heart is still greater than the things which do surround it, able, if fair and noble things were not, to create them out of its own wealth."

"The whole," resumed Philip, "interprets to us the parts, more surely than the parts the whole, so that to judge of any great or good thing fairly we must have the whole before us, we must even presuppose it, in order to a just conception of the parts. To get a true idea of any character or system, we must seize, as Neander advises, upon its higher *forming* element; I would even go further than he does, and say that we cannot understand the Actual of a character or system without in some degree entering into its Ideal, that to which it naturally tends.

For there is in all things an Ideal, a Divine principle, revealing itself in spite of contradictory elements, something which it would fain be, yet which it only *can* be in a sudden, transitory flash; as an ordinary face will in some moment of satisfied affection, of exalted feeling, be transfigured into beauty and nobleness. Who has not known moments when the whole of a friend's heart has been in his looks and voice; moments in which a lifetime of goodness and affection has revealed itself, perhaps at the touch of some slight and apparently casual circumstance? And I think it is for this that the general heart of humanity has been ever disposed to set such a seemingly disproportionate value upon sudden acts of self-sacrifice and heroic daring, deeds like those of the Chevalier d'Assas, — that though they occupy but a moment, *the whole of a life is in them.* Moments of sudden emergency leave, it is true, no time for choice, for reflection, for much that makes an action morally great; but they are like the lightning's flash across the spirit, bringing out its lineaments in clear and awful distinctness.

Such deeds give us a great soul speaking in its unguarded sleep, showing us what it truly is. And the less exalted aspects of life have also at a lower level their consistency; the whole tree is in its every leaf; the whole body, soul, and spirit of man is in some degree in his every action. When a person is known intimately, each of his movements and gestures bears a characteristic stamp; even a garment he has worn becomes instinct with life and individuality; it suggests the familiar face, it is filled out with the well-known form. This, we say, *belongs* to him. So may God be discerned in Humanity, so may Christ be seen in his Church."

"And yet," I said, "as regards this last great subject, how poor, insufficient, and therefore practically inefficient, are our conceptions! The Bible, as De Maistre says, clearly intimates that the Church is as necessary to Christ as he is to the Church; *it* is emphatically the fulness of him who filleth all in all.* This wonderful saying shows us that *unity* is the *end* of all the Divine plans with regard to us. Even Christ is

* Ephesians i. 23.

only complete through the building up of his body, the Church: we are complete in him; he is completed in us. His words are not only 'You in me,' but also, 'I in you': the Head of the great body says not to any one of his members, 'I have no need of thee.' The Epistles are full of references to the organic life of the Church; the building 'up of this breathing house not made with hands' is spoken of as a gradual work, — a work which moves altogether, if it moves at all; *the whole body*, St. Paul tells us, grows through that which *every* joint supplieth. They also testify to a common, a transferable spiritual property; a bread sometimes of affliction, sometimes of rejoicing, of which 'all are partakers.' 'If we be afflicted,' says St. Paul, 'it is for your salvation *which is wrought* in the enduring of the same sufferings which we also suffer, or whether we be comforted, it is for your consolation and salvation.' 'We also,' he says again, 'are weak in Christ, but we shall live by the power of God toward you.' He speaks further of individual poverty, which tends, and not indirectly, to the general wealth, 'We are fools for Christ's sake, but ye are wise in Christ; we are weak, but ye are strong'; and intimates that the prayers of 'many helping together' will bring upon Timothy and himself a blessing for which 'many' will return thanks. Nay, he does not even limit this reciprocal interchange, this mutual interest and help, to the members of the human family, whether militant on earth or rejoicing in heaven. How many of his deep sayings, such as Col. i. 20, Eph. i. 10, imply that the benefits of Christ's great sacrifice have a bearing *beyond* that family, such as bring it into relations with other and spiritual orders of existence. Who knows upon what worlds, what systems, Christian prayer and effort even now *tells?* It was not to men only that St. Paul's commission was addressed. He preached among them the unsearchable riches of Christ, *to the intent* that the manifold wisdom of God might be made known to principalities and powers in heavenly places through the Church which was thus founding. See Eph. iii. 10. 'The fellowship of the mystery' he there speaks of is *a mystery of fellowship*, one that fellowship only can admit us to."

"You have quoted De Maistre," said Philip, thoughtfully; "do not these expressions, at least in the sense in which you receive them, —and I do not see how they will bear any other, — come very near his favorite theory of *reversibility?*"

"Not nearer," I returned, "than Baxter comes, when he speaks of his own times a truth that holds good of all: 'It is because we have so few high saints among us, that we have so many low sinners,' and not nearer certainly than life itself comes. In the meanest thing of every day, no man liveth, no man dieth unto himself, so inwrapt and interfolded are human destinies in the continual action and reaction that goes on through life. And if it is thus with the outward course of things, dealing with what is material and secular, how much more so in that great unseen order where finer springs are touched to surer issues, the spiritual life of man! The Christian is one who in work and life and prayer 'strengthens himself' for the sake of many; he belongs consciously to a kingdom in which there is nothing unrelated."

"True," said Philip, "and a time comes to the soul when individualism becomes cramping, narrowing; when we feel conscious that we cannot breathe and move freely either in work or prayer, except through the universal organic whole."

"What," I resumed, "is Christianity itself, *but living to the whole instead of living to the part?* It gives the heart Christ instead of self for its spring and centre; it says unto it, 'Behold the Man'; not Paul now, nor Apollos, not even Christ Jesus himself as a man; if we have known him as such in a merely personal relation, we know him as such no more, but as the great High-Priest *standing before God in the place of humanity*, whose sins, whose griefs, and burdens, he has taken upon himself, first-born among many brethren. *Ecce Homo!* the earliest impression I ever received of Christ was from a colored engraving, with these words beneath it; I remember distinctly the place where it used to hang; the crown of thorns, the bleeding forehead, the kind and sorrowful countenance. I remember, as a very little child, asking what the two Latin words meant; how long have I been in learning their full meaning! Protestantism has done much for the world by its consistent testimony to moral responsibility, by its faithful education of the individual spirit; but from the exclusive stress it lays upon what is individual and interior, it bears but feeble witness to one organic spiritual unity; to the fact that we, being many members, are one body in Christ. Roman Catholicism has loudly proclaimed this unity; it has been its lot to keep and to transmit a secret which it has not apparently understood. It has testified that the human race, whether in Adam or in Christ, is *one;* but it has missed the contingent necessary truth, *that because we are one*, because we possess organic life, that life will assume different manifestations. All that lives *grows*, and grows after its own fashion; it is only that which is *made*, ready made, which can be reproduced a thousand times over, in any age or in any clime, in the order and pattern desired. This truth, Popery, waiting from age to age to devour the man-child of mental and spiritual freedom so soon as it should be born, has ignored, has trampled under foot, and even yet, wherever Popery continues in the ascendant there can be no harmonious development, no free, progressive life, none of that mutual help and enlightenment, each supplying what each needs, which is the soul and life-breath of Church fellowship. Stiff with its own infallibility, the Church of Rome sits before Christendom like the enchanter before the lady in Comus, ready to chain up its nerves in alabaster."

"It is not hard, I think," said Philip, "to contemplate Catholicity apart from Popery."

"And in that case," I continued, "not hard to see how Catholicity still holds to her heart this flower, *the unity of man!* Often has its fragrance, as that of a flower cast forth to perish, come across me in lonely and uncultured places, making the desert glad; *here* only I find it planted in the garden of the Lord, and drawing round it, as thick as bees in summer, every tender and hopeful thought. There are in the world many kinds of voices, and none of them without signification; wandering, wind-awakened tones seeming to die upon the air that calls them forth, — *Liberty*, *Equality*, *Fraternity*, the sound of a trumpet and the voice of words. But what has it been to me to recognize *this* voice, dear in the poet's song, the patriot's vision, — sweet even in its most bitter accents, wrung from the heart of some stern, solitary thinker grown desperate over this world's wrong; what has it been to me to hear it speaking to us no longer in parables, but showing us plainly of the Father? *What but the awakening into a blissful dream?* The intellect has many illusions; but the dreams of the heart come true, because the instinct of the heart is prophetic. Catholicity, or, in other words, apostolic Christianity, is the fulfilment of the heart's best dream; it contemplates humanity as one, and as such aims at its restoration; as One fallen in Adam, as One redeemed in Christ; it works ever towards the whole, its task is to bring back the One to the One, humanity to

God. It looks also upon the individual man as one, a being spiritual, rational, and sensitive, and as such provides him with food convenient for him ; it gives us no manna of mere spirituality, angels' food, thin and unsatisfying ; but sets before us bread,—the bread of which Christ said, 'It is my flesh, which I will give for the life of the world.' It does not throw the whole strain of spiritual life upon a moment, a feeling, a movement of the heart, of which, at some other moment and under some other feeling, the heart itself may doubt ; it receives us while yet passive ; unconscious of either good or evil, it takes us up within its arms to bless us. It makes not upon the heart that continual, exhaustive demand, 'Faith, faith,' but lays within it faith's deep foundation ; it declares of our spiritual Zion that this Man was born there, and proclaims that the Highest doth even now inhabit her ; it brings forth the headstone with shoutings of 'Grace, grace.'"

"Catholicity," said Philip, "is great in this, that while it leaves within it room and scope for the most ardent personal aspiration, for the closest individual union with Christ that the heart can claim, *it does not leave the heart to itself*, to its own experiences, its own aspirations. It regards humanity as a field which the Lord hath blessed, as a soil where the good seed is already sown, and needs but to be quickened and developed. It brings Christ into the foreground of spiritual life, and lets life root itself round his life. It lifts before the soul its great Object, that which alone can lift it up; through rite, through creed, through symbol, it brings the human spirit into neighborhood with Christ, and lets it grow up gradually unto him."

"Catholicity," I continued, "requires nothing from the individual but sincerity; its congregation, like that of the Israelites, are all holy *de jure;* all, until reprobate and self-excluded, are citizens of no mean city. They have nothing to prove, nothing to keep up before men; let but their light burn unto God, it may take care of its own shining. It is easy to see how different a position the individual holds in communities where the test of fellowship is inward, as among the Baptist and other of the stricter

Protestant sects, where membership in Christ is not admitted until the individual has gone through a conscious spiritual change. There, even in the countenance, you can often trace a painful constraint and self-consciousness, as of persons committed to a standard of feeling which they may not be at all times equal to maintain. The spirit of man, we all know,

> 'Is competent to win
> Heights which it is not competent to keep.' "

" The heart of man," said Philip, " is too weak to be forever self-regulating. Christ is to his Church what the sun is to the world,— its great universal clock, to which the whole system is so adapted, that a flower opens and shuts to the same law by which the heavenly bodies move. In Catholicity there is little of stimulus and pressure; little to fear from those sharp collapses which are their inevitable result. It lifts the strain from self to Christ; it is evidently made for man; *suited for him as he is now*. But is there not also something beautiful in the Protestant ideal of a Church, striving as it does to antedate the time when God's people shall be all righteous? Something in it, too, which answers to that deep-seated longing for inner purity, that desire after perfection, which must, as things are at present constituted, ever defeat itself, and yet ever form part of true Christian consciousness? . . . . . And what, after all," resumed Philip, thoughtfully, "is a sect but the recognition of a Church? the effort to tighten the bonds which, in the great national churches, are apt to hang so loosely as to be scarcely felt? There is something in Christianity, if we examine its history closely, which always for its full development requires an inner circle, a church within the church. It has found this in the Sect, the Order; it finds it too, in many an English parish, in a humble, healthful, almost unsuspected shape, in the work which, under good organization, grows up naturally about the Church. I once lived in a large manufacturing village, where a numerously attended Sunday school became such a spiritual centre, and possessed all the attractive, binding energy I speak of; the more thoughtful persons of every class being drawn out as teachers, meeting the clergyman for prayer and reading of the Scriptures, with an especial reference to the common work; while *these*, in their turn, influenced the more seriously disposed young people, to whom the care of the very little ones was committed. I often recall these younger teachers, factory boys and girls, some of them even unable to read very fluently, yet most successful in the management of their infant classes. How attached they were to their little pupils, visiting them when sick, and taking them various small comforts! How affectionate to their elder friends! That was the only place," said Philip, smiling, "where I was ever serenaded! My boys knew my favorite hymns, and used to sing them under my window in summer evenings. All things seemed to unite us more closely, — the mirth of our yearly festivals; the happy deaths of some among us; even the sorrowful fallings away of some that at first did run well; the losses belonging to every great gain; the disappointments inseparable from every real work:

in all things we were as members, rejoicing and suffering *together*. . . . . .

"Again, in large towns you will find an interest in the great Christian societies, such as those connected with foreign missions, or active local work among the destitute and fallen, working the same effect in calling forth the more intimate spiritual affections. There is no such firm, such attaching bond, as that of prayer and a common work for Christ. *A common work tends to a common life*, fuller than the individual can ever live. How can one, being alone, be warm? Do you remember the almost secret associations established during the last century, a period of great license in the Nation, and of great coldness in the Church, 'for the reformation of manners'?—societies so humble in their scope, and so quiet in their action, that it is now difficult to gather any exact account of them. They are only to be traced back in the works which have followed them, not only discernible in 'sweeter manners, purer laws,' but in their direct historical connection with the great religious and missionary societies which now go through the length and breadth of our land. It is evident that our spiritual and our natural life are alike in this, that each needs, from time to time, to be refreshed, quickened, *by something not within ourselves.* We require the reciprocal action of heart upon heart, life calling forth life. Even in natural things there is no fulness except through participation; and I myself have been long persuaded that we do not fully live unto Christ except through mutual communion. How significant is that saying of St. John's, 'If we walk in the light, as he is in the light, we have fellowship one with another'! And there is surely a mystery in our Saviour's words, 'Where two or three are gathered together in my name, there am I in the midst of them.' The genius of the old Dispensation was individual, God speaking to the soul of patriarch and prophet, and receiving for answer, 'Here am *I*.' The new Covenant knows little of solitary manifestations. When Jesus is to be transfigured, he taketh with him Peter and James and John; when the Holy Spirit is to be given, the disciples are all assembled with one accord, in one place."

As I looked at Philip, and saw how he warmed and almost grew with his great theme, I was reminded of the sermon some mediæval divine preached upon it to the text, "Philip *and* Bartholomew," the last-named of these two disciples being never mentioned in Holy Writ except in connection with the former.

"And there is yet another side," he continued, "from which it is well to look at this subject. In the frequent darkness and deadness of the human spirit, how strange, how powerfully re-enforcing is the influence of true communion! You, I know, from some cheerfulness of my voice and aspect, find it hard to think of me but as strong and equal; you do not easily believe that I, like yourself, am visited by moods in which earth seems desolate, and heaven even geographically a long way off, with all lines of communication broken. At such seasons how does one desire a gale, a *lift;* to be taken up like a little bird under the wing of a strong eagle, and brought nearer the sun! But does it ever come to you to suffer under an anguish of unbelief, of a rational, or apparently rational, irresistible kind, when some dark, besieging thought, which the soul can neither answer nor dismiss, comes forward in a form so fixed and definite, that reason seems spell-bound before it; and though the heart and spirit protest, it is so feebly as to appear almost like consent? This state of mind is, I think, the hardest of all to bear, because it is one which leaves the soul no place to flee unto; it is hunted from one desolation to another. I shall never forget a day of this kind last summer; a day outwardly of golden warmth and sweetness; of quiet, too; for I was staying in my old parish in the country. In the evening a few of my young men, Sunday scholars and pupil-teachers, with whom, five years ago, I had spent many a happy, well-remembered hour, came in to see and welcome me. It was an effort to me, under such circumstances, to appear so glad to see them as I should naturally have felt; a still greater effort to pass into any intercourse beyond that of kindly chat and greetings; yet I made it, and we had reading and talk and prayer together as of old. I cannot describe to you the effect this little hour of prayer and of true communion had upon me; even like that of the bursting of a dark thunder-cloud, and it affected me in this way. *I felt* that Christ and the Holy Spirit, regeneration, and the blessed, glorious hopes that the Gospel holds out to us, are at any rate as *real* as the gulfs set between man and all that he seems made for, — sin, indifference, despair, — as real as all that had perplexed me; these, too, are *facts*, historic, living facts, met and answered by the heart to which they are addressed, meeting our deep need. At that time I could not have prayed alone; a wind from the desert, a dry, searching breath, would have swept my words; I needed to pass out of my own soul, wasted and girt with fire, into the freedom of less harassed spirits. Seasons like these have made me think much on the subject of communion and its deep inward blessedness. To know, as I do, looking over the country at this moment, till my eye rests upon the remote edge of the horizon, that there is a poor man or woman living there who believes, and loves, and prays, makes me a happier, *abler* Christian. To borrow an illustration from nature, do you know that ice cannot change to water, or water to steam, until the temperature of the whole has been raised to a certain level? We cannot raise the temperature of a thawing mass of ice until we have thawed the whole; until *all* the ice has passed into water, all the water into steam. Any heat short of the amount required to produce these changes becomes latent and disappears; *it is absorbed in producing these changes.* How much Christian energy and love disappears, sinks below the surface, in this way, depressed by the low level of the surrounding atmosphere.

"As the world is, the few earnest Christians scattered here and there in it, one in a family, a few in a city, are enough to keep the mass from freezing; but their life, we may say, *is spent in keeping up their life:*

> 'A flower that, bold and patient, thrusts its way
> Through stony chinks, lives on from day to day,
> But little shows of fragrance or of bloom.'

How sorely in social life will the want of generous and exalted aims, the absence of lofty and kindly traditions, affect a whole community! It is hard to be always in opposition; even the nobler mind will in some degree succumb to what it continually meets, becoming, like the dyer's hand, 'subdued to that it works in.' How different it is when heart is met by heart, and hand helped out by hand, as is sometimes, if too seldom, seen in a household that have among them but one heart and one mind, and *that* the mind which was in Christ Jesus! A home wherein earthly affections, without losing their characteristic sweetness, have been made to bear the image of the heavenly; where love between child and parent, between husband and wife, has been transfigured into a more perfect likeness; where to brotherly kindness, a natural bond which is strong, but not always tender, has been 'added' the spiritual tie of charity. What is there too hard for such a family to undertake and to accomplish?"

Philip took from his pocket-book a little prayer, which he had found, he told me, in a very old collection:—

A Prayer for Christ's Kingdom.

"*But how unthankful I am, and sorrowless, Lord, thou knowest, for my heart is not hid from thee. O be merciful unto me, good Father, and grant me the Spirit of thy children, to reveal unto me my ignorance of thy kingdom, my poverty, and perversity, that I may lament the same, and daily labor for thy help and thy Holy Spirit to suppress the kingdom of sin in myself and others. Again, grant me that same, thy Holy Spirit, to reveal to me thy kingdom of power, grace, and glory; to kindle mine affections towards it; to renew me more and more; to reign in me as in a piece of thy kingdom; to give me to desire, to pray, and to labor for thy kingdom, both to myself and others; that the power, excellence, and majesty of thy kingdom may be known among men.*"

We were both long silent. Philip resumed: "Do you not think that the secret of the extraordinary hold of Methodism upon the English poor lies in the strict and intimate communion which forms so essential a part of it? Before John Wesley commenced that great revival of spiritual religion which was blest to whole counties, towns, villages, and the fruits of which are still to be found, not only in many a remote and many a populous district in England, but in America, Sweden, and almost the whole of Protestant Christendom, he describes himself as having walked many miles to see and discourse with 'a serious person,' who said to him, 'You must either find companions or make them; there is no such thing as going to heaven alone.' Methodism is eminently social; its idea is that of journeying Zionwards in companies, gathering as they go; husbands, wives, friends, servants, little ones, 'leaving not a hoof behind'; its activities are ever aggressive, its sympathies ever widening;

'We weep for those who weep below,
And burdened, for the afflicted sigh;
The various forms of human woe
Attract our softest sympathy.' "

"True," I said, "I know no more singular contrast than to turn, as I have lately done, from Wesley's hymns to those of Augustus Toplady, in their way as fine as any in our language, but admitting us into a world in which there is God and the individual soul only; no breath or whisper to tell of any other creature, the hymn goes up straight like a flame or dart;

it is Jacob's ladder into heaven without either man or angel ascending or descending the shining stairs."

"Have you seen," continued Philip, "a book called *Ploughing and Sowing*, by a lady deeply interested in the improvement of the boys and young men employed on the great farms in Yorkshire, a class hitherto neglected, and exposed to the peculiar evils which arise from close association, when, as under the Bothy system in Scotland, the humanizing influences of family life are withdrawn. She, the daughter of a clergyman, speaks of Methodism in the part of England she lives in — the East Riding of Yorkshire — as being a mitigated form of dissent, involving little feeling of separation from the Church, and no ill-will towards it. She says it is the only *real* religion of the working classes; to be 'brought in' and 'to join a society' is with them synonymous with true earnestness in religion, and the conversion of the soul to God. When you are told that such a one is 'religious,' you always find on inquiry that it means he has joined a society; a well-conducted person who has *not* done so will be spoken of as being 'very good for a worldly man.' A boy said to the writer, 'All the folks at our farm are religious except me, and I'm going to be so very soon.' The boys, influenced for good by this lady — herself a firm Churchwoman — seem, with little more than one exception, to become Wesleyans, as if it had been the natural fruit of her admonitions; they give as one reason, 'You see, what with class-meetings, and prayer-meetings, and preachings, Wesleyans have so much more *means* * than Church people.' I know well how much is involved in this last statement, for I have so often, in talking to devout poor people, found that it was the need of a closer warmth of spiritual sympathy, and this need only, that had drawn them from the Church to Methodism, or some other form of dissent. They will tell you that when they first became interested in spiritual things, anxious inquirers after salvation, they found no one in the Church to whom they could open their hearts; the clergyman

* I. e. "means of grace."

removed from familiar intercourse, fellow Church people of their own class indifferent and unenlightened."

"True," I said, "but how much, too, of the strength of Methodism is to be found in its *directness.* As Napoleon in his grand secret of battle would accumulate all his force upon one point in the enemy's ranks, instead of diffusing it from line to line in a series of desultory attacks, so does this teaching press home upon the soul the one point that it either is or is not turned to God, and urge it, if still reluctant and wavering, to take at once that self-renunciating, self-dedicatory step. Surely there is great, inestimable gain in thus bringing a soul into a felt relation with its God, in making the first step in spiritual progress to consist in a real conscious transaction between the soul and him; and yet I know that in this very directness there may be danger; the risk of recoil that follows upon extreme tension, the possibility of mistaking a spasm for a birth."

"These are dangers," returned Philip, "inherent in every system that makes conversion the *beginning* of life unto God; they cease to exist when this great fact of spiritual experience is received, as in apostolical teaching, *in its connection with other facts*, when it is recognized as growing out of an already established relation between the soul and God."

"You would then preach conversion," I said, "as being not the soul's birth, but its awakening; you would set it forth as the turning-point in the *direction* of the soul's journey, — a turning, be it ever remembered, not always needed, for the great family of Christ should surely number with it many 'plants grown up in their youth,' requiring no violent transformation; and yet to the great mass of professing Christians a needed change, a change of purpose and of affection worked by the Holy Spirit upon the human soul, a change of which it *must* in some degree be conscious."

"Yes," resumed Philip, "as surely as it would be conscious of any earthly love, or hope, or joy. 'He that believeth hath the witness in himself.' And here we touch upon another secret of the strength of Methodism, that it brings the great and comforting *reality* of pardon and acceptance, the love and peace and joy of believing, into far stronger relief than is usually done in Church teaching. When we consider the state of our lapsed masses, the great gulf their modes of life and thought have fixed between them and all methods of regular instruction and gradual training, we learn to bless a teaching that applies such powerful stimulants, such strong consolations to the soul; that rouses it from the deadly lethargy of sense and sin, and sends it out, perhaps, to weep in solitary places, to 'wrestle,' as the poor Methodist expresses it, with its God; that lifts it from the conflict into the clear sunshine of peace and hope and rejoicing; that leaves it at the feet of Jesus, saying, 'I have found him whom my soul loveth.' Sudden conversions, with the ecstatic warmth of feeling that follows upon them, are derided, but only by those who know, even as regards natural things, little of the secret powers, the reserved forces of the human spirit, and are unaware that in the depths of ignorant, and hardened, and weary, and distracted souls there is still a Strength, blind and fettered like that of Samson, needing a shock to set it free. 'The kingdom of heaven suffereth violence, and the violent take it by force.' Methodism has entered into the heart of this saying."

"More deeply, you think, than the Church has done?"

"Far more deeply. And yet," continued Philip, "is not the Church, as all-inclusive, able to provide for all exceptional as well as for all ordinary wants? Should *any* exigency, whether spiritual or social, whether of the age or of the individual spirit, find her unprepared to meet and minister unto it? In the wholeness of Catholicity she possesses each gift, each doctrine that, taken in isolation, makes, as it were, the peculiar treasure of the Separated Communions; she possesses them, but in how many cases as treasure *hid!* her best things, as in careful households, being too often kept as things of state, rather than used as things of daily service and delight. What does she need, however, but, even like the scriptural householder, to *bring forth* out of her treasure things new and old; what does she need but to take up from the heart her ancient, true confession, 'I believe in the Holy Ghost, the Lord and Giver of life'? Has this third Divine Person been *as yet* worshipped and glorified among us together with the Father and the Son? And yet where shall we meet with a more implicit avowal of dependence upon its Mighty Agency than is to be found in our liturgy? Our collects have among them but one speech and language; and this is the confession of natural weakness, joined with the reliance upon supernatural help. 'O God, forasmuch as without thee we are not able to please thee; mercifully grant that thy Holy Spirit may in all things direct and rule our hearts through Jesus Christ our Lord.' When I consider these inspired prayers, and remember how long they have been the life-breath of our National Church, I can but compare her with the Bride in Canticles, who said, 'I sleep, but my heart waketh.' Her Lord, however, cometh that he may awake her out of sleep. We have long had Eldad and Medad prophesying in the camp, fire has broken out in strange remote places, and all that we see within and without us leads us, with a writer of our day, to claim as the world's chiefest blessing a revival in the Catholic Church. Of this revival there are now many signs, and even if we still miss something of an inward spiritual glow, the baptism of the Holy Ghost and of fire, the very statistics of our Church are cheering. She has lighted her candle, and begun to sweep her house diligently; soon, perhaps, in a closer union with her Head, in a fuller communion with his earthly members, she may call in her friends and neighbors to rejoice with her."

Philip was silent; after a long pause I said: "Will not this revival, in becoming more definite, take the form of a deepened appreciation of the blessings which the Church has held perhaps in a loose grasp, held out with a cold hand, but always *held?* These will become her *gifts*, her treasures, rightly divided, lovingly distributed among her children, who will become aware of their true value through rational and spiritual recognition. I place these two words together advisedly, for *it is the irrational which is above all else the unspiritual;* we shall ever find that the least rational view, or in other words the most superstitious one, of any divine ordinance, is invariably the one which least helps to spirituality. As the mere formalist, who values form for its own sake, and would *bind* it where it does not grow, is the one person in the world who the least appreciates form's deep significance as being the result of an inner law, the expression which life naturally takes, so is it the person who looks to Baptism or to the Lord's Supper to save him, who blindly and ignorantly accepts the rites of Christianity as an end, the one who least of all enters into their inappreciable value as means."

"And as with its rites," said Philip, "so with its great institutions; it is those who understand what a Church is, who are the least likely to rest in it, or in anything short of Him to whom it leads. And even so with the Priesthood; I sometimes feel as if this Order, coexistent with Christianity itself, sometimes unduly exalted, sometimes unduly depressed, had yet to show forth its true beauty, and the general Church yet to learn its true value. How interesting is it in its connection with national and with family life; it is impossible, even where this is made an express aim, to detach these bonds, —

> 'As with the priest, so with the people;
> As with the people, so with the priest.'

Their standard of dignity, their level of purity, must be ever one; the fire of the altar is always brought from the household hearth, the hearth kindled from the altar. '*It is from the earth itself that the salt of the earth is taken.*' The name of priest has been desecrated till the very word, in some degree, carries with it the idea of something either spiritually despotic, or dryly ecclesiastical and official; yet what word, what thought is in reality so tender as that of a Man, *brought nearer than other men are, at once to man and to God?* When applied to our Lord himself, no other of his offices seems to bring and to keep him beside us in so intimate and human a relation as that of his 'unchangeable Priesthood.' 'He is a Priest forever'; one separate from sinners and undefiled; and yet, through this very separation, drawn into the closest union with Humanity. Christ, when on earth, was upbraided for his freedom and accessibility. 'Behold this man receiveth sinners, and eateth with them'; and yet, like Joseph, the very type of bounty and brotherhood, he is one 'that is separated from his brethren,' drawing their souls after him, while he withdraws from their presence. The heart desires one who is greater, purer, kinder, *freer* than itself, one standing aloof from its conscious falseness, its self-confessed littleness; therefore is Christ, *because he is lifted up*, able to draw all men unto him; to draw as none other can do, close to Humanity, and to draw it close to him. And as with the Master, so with his true disciples; there is ever something sacrificial in the Christian's life, something which will ofttimes compel him to 'put a space' between his own soul and the souls upon which his desires and prayers are set; he must free himself from every disturbing element, and be content to depart from his brethren in many things and at many seasons, so that he may abide with them forever in a truer, deeper fellowship than any which is founded upon the conditions of an earthly amity. Unsecularity is the strength and glory of the Christian Priesthood; the Agency they deal with is one which, like that of some great mechanic force, must work *apart* from that on which it is brought to bear, — its power is lost in conformity, it lives in transformation, in renewal; it is content to die to its own individual hopes and interests, so that, falling within the wide field of Humanity, it may in dying bring forth *much fruit.*

YET a little while longer, and Philip and I must part; we saw before us the point at which our paths would break, never perhaps to be reunited, for the last command of One long loved and followed, "Go teach all nations," had ever been precious to Philip's spirit; he was now about to obey its leading, and to go forth to fields of labor as yet unbroken, but scarcely more arduous than those in which he had toiled so long. "*Even unto this last*" had been the motto of Philip's life; he had chosen his portion among the things that all others reject, and in now devoting himself to the most wronged and most benighted among the nations, he did but follow out the sure and secret instinct which had ever drawn him towards the forlorn, the degraded, and the despised. He sailed for Africa in a few weeks. And now that the time of his departure drew nearer, it seemed that our hearts drew closer, so would the idea of that solemn, perhaps life-long parting, pervade and deepen all our intercourse, and cast a shadow round us, — a shadow like that green twilight of the summer woods, which is but the light grown tender.

And the idea of that utter separation brought with it a strange feeling across my mind; as if Philip were already severed from my life and all familiar things belonging to it, I seemed even now to view him apart from circumstance, apart from his bodily presence; he was near to me, and yet afar, like one who has been long dead. Even while we talked together, my mind would sometimes detach itself from the subject we were engaged with, to occupy itself with him, till all that he was grew up before me in clear and defined outline. O that I could but retain some one of these hasty gestures, some one of these sudden, unlooked-for turns of thought in which the deep sincerity of his nature was revealed, — that I could bring it back to me, and Philip with it, in days that were yet to come! Yet it was doubtless expedient for me that he should go away, for man doth not live by bread alone, not even by that which best nourishes his heart and spirit, but by every word that proceedeth out of the mouth of God.

And that word was now Farewell. We spent much of our remaining time together; we spoke often of his future work, and even when we did not speak or consciously think of it, the idea of Africa — of its burning sky and sands, its strange and glowing forms of life, its vast undeveloped resources — of all that makes it a land of wonder and mystery — was so far present to us as to tinge our conversation with something of an unearthly, ideal character. How clearly I can recall those days, which were passed by the sea-shore, the sea which was so soon to part us; how we would gaze upon it from the rocks, or still looking over it, lie for hours upon the grassy cliffs, and yet keep within our hearts a sense of the rich inland country that lay behind these green, desolate ridges, thick with farms, and villages, and little peaceful towns. Even now, through a thin belt of wood in the distance, I could see the yellow, sword-like gleam of barley flashing in the sunshine, — for it was Autumn, and earth wore upon her breast the rich and russet gold that is more goodly than all she hides so deep within it. The very air was still and fruitful, it seemed to ripen our fancies upon it along with all that was now ripening, our words seemed to linger on it lightly, as the loosened leaves will linger and float awhile before their quiet, unmarked fall. Then we would let the broad ocean woo our thoughts into infinity; we sent them across it fearlessly, for all things seemed to beckon us onwards; the line of silver that spread over the wide glittering bay, the white sea-birds that rose and fell with the waves, — even the dun sails of the fishing vessels, touched by the light of evening with a tawny splendor, seemed also to be winged messengers, coming to us we knew not whence, and taking us we cared not whither.

"How the sea," I remarked, "seems to round a landscape, to *finish* it, and yet to make it illimitable, just as our life is rounded by eternity. What strength and gladness too is there in its voice, something in its very awfulness which makes it facile and companionable. Its continual movement without weariness, its flash, its smile, the ever-changing music of its monotony, — a monotony too vast to be oppressive, — always gives me a feeling intimately connected with that of our future life, so that it seems strange to me to read in Scripture that 'there shall be no more sea.'"

"It is hard," answered Philip, "to imagine that there will be anything left out of our future life which is beautiful and good in this one. Once I was easily satisfied with the idea of heaven; I asked for nothing more than to be *there;* now I have grown solicitous about the nature of our happiness. How strange it is," he continued, "that there should be in some lives this order, *first* that which is spiritual, and then that which is natural. Yet so it has been with mine, and thus, judging from what has at various times fallen from you, with your own also. I feel now no longer able to contemplate life under the strict and absolute aspect under which it once appeared to me, as being a place of discipline, a training-ground for spiritual perfection, a way, in short, to a higher and more complete life. Now I can see grandeur, beauty, even divinity, in things that do not minister to any of these objects, — that even appear to lead in far opposite directions ; greatness, even Pagan greatness, irresistibly attracts my spirit, and at times I feel my soul drawn out of itself with a love that is almost passion for universal truth and beauty, 'those things which are eternal because they are.' When such moods as these are upon me, I sometimes wonder if heaven will be the resurrection of our life, *of our whole life*, if it will be the bloom-time and expansion, not only of our spiritual being, but of all those germs of natural delight which seem unable to unfold here. How much is there in life to which life is itself unfriendly! How much that must fall off, wither, perish; how many first loves of the heart and soul and spirit, whose destiny is written in their beauty, *they are fated to die young*. Yet how fair and exalted a thing, under its happier conditions, is natural life! in its illusions, which are but truths *anticipated* in the clear second-sight of the soul; in its elations, when the heart dilates and lifts up the whole of life along with it! I discern in the human heart an innate love of splendor and distinction, showing itself in ordinary life, in what is vulgar and ostentatious, yet in truth, I think, connected with our higher nature, in fact, a reminiscence of it, such as a high-born child, stolen from his home in youth, might feel awakening within him at the sight of grandeur.

> 'The poorest man
> Is in the poorest thing superfluous';

human nature always appears, as Shakespeare observes, to claim something beyond what it positively needs; how readily will it, even under its most depressed conditions, respond to the call of what is gay and festal; how willingly will it let its hidden poetry bloom, if it be but for half a day! Our very Sunday-school festivals would not be what they are to us but for the bright flags and banners waving above our little procession, our music, our triumphal arches, our wreaths and pictures on the walls of the school-room. You know," continued Philip, "what my daily life is; how little there is in it to minister to the instinct I am now speaking of; yet it is strange how my dreams will carry me among scenes of more than earthly loveliness; how all within me, which possibly the day represses, seems to culminate in some vision of enchantment. Yet it is no cold, metallic heaven to which the gate of sleep admits me, no steely splendor, no glittering, wearying glory, no 'Jerusalem the golden,' as so many of our hymns describe it, making both the eyes and heart ache; all that I find there is tender, human, satisfying; its very light, clothing all things with splendor, comes warm and rose-flushed through the heart."

Philip paused, and resumed abruptly: "I should like to tell you one of these dreams, though to do so will be like drawing out one of these delicate films of sea-weed from the pool, where it is spreading in such beauty, — all the glow and lustre will fade when it leaves the water, — even so with my dream while I try to put it into words;

> 'What marks hath blessedness;
> What characters whereby it may be told?'

I do not remember the beginning of my dream, or how I came to find myself in a smooth, grassy opening in the very depths of a forest; the thick wood stood round it in unbroken masses, and made a wall of verdure, that gave a feeling of security without the sense of gloom, so wide was the clearing, so broad the sunshine of the summer noonday that seemed to concentrate its light upon it; yet it was light without glare, a calm, steadfast light, like that of a loving eye, too friendly to confuse or dazzle. I seemed to be seated at a table, round which men of noble, even princely bearing were gathered in deep conference, in which I myself was a sharer, with One of middle age and majestic aspect, who seemed to be their leader: in their dress and language was a trace of something that severed them from our present times, and yet I knew not to what age of the world to refer it. At a little distance from the table a boy richly dressed sang to the lute, in tones so clear and ringing, that while I slept both the music and the words seemed *visible* to me, such ravishment did they pour within my soul. The table was spread for a banquet, heaped with costly plate, and fruits, and wine; all showed splendor and profusion, and around it was boundless hilarity, chastened, I thought, but not checked by the presence of some lofty aim, some common ground of hope and joy and triumph, that shed I know not what moral charm over the whole scene. Each brow I looked on was as open as the sunshine that streamed above us; eye met eye, and heart answered heart. Then the scene changed, and I was wandering amid the deep glades of the forest, in the warm stillness of the afternoon. As I strayed onwards I met scattered parties of children, searching for flowers and berries; they put their little hands within mine, they drew me down beside them on the grassy path to tell me some secret all important to their childish hearts, and in the telling they put their arms about my neck and kissed me, with the kisses of the soul, closer than anything can ever come on earth. A little farther on I met bands of youths and maidens, crowned with flowers, and singing as they descended a steep, rocky path that led into the deep and now darkening ravines of the forest. They, too, greeted me as one who had been long known, yet in their greeting, I thought, was less of recognition than of affinity, close and intimate as had been the kisses of the children. I wandered with them towards a castle, now shining in the last evening glow. O, how rich was that sunset, purple and a clear amber, that strove long for the mastery, and at last fused in a divided victory. It had grown dusk when I reached the castle; my bright companions had vanished, but I heard their distant voices; and still far, far away, that of the singer singing to his lute. Now, methought, I walked in the sober twilight with one who has been ever most dear to me, but from whom the pressure of life has long parted me; life that can sever hearts far more utterly than death.

We paced together up and down a mossy terrace; we spoke of many things, both of trifling and of serious interest, as friends do who meet after the separation of a day. I did not forget the circumstances that had seemed to estrange us, but they seemed scarcely worth alluding to; we were now reunited, all was accounted for, all was natural and right. I awoke in a sort of rapture, my spirit bathed in a conscious fulness of rest and satisfaction such as not even my dream had given; a state described by the prophet when he says, '*After this*, I awoke and beheld, and lo! my sleep was sweet unto me.' Slowly *I awoke out of this also* into the gray November morning—"

"And mourned, I suppose, to find it was but a dream?"

"No," returned Philip, his color heightening; "you will wonder when I tell you the thought that crept over me with that blank, chill dawn; bitterness was in my soul, and along with it a sort of contempt for the Life hereafter; not even *there*, I thought, shall I behold such beings, noble, beautiful, and loving as these that sleep has brought around me. O, how dim and colorless, how tame and uniform, did the Christian heaven at that moment seem!"

"But why," I said, "should heaven seem so?"

"Why, indeed," returned Philip, laughing; "I only say that it *did* seem so."

"Perhaps," I answered, "because you were thinking of it as it appeared to the ancient world. The blank, shadowy existence before which Achilles and Iphigenia preferred *life*, even were it that of a slave 'toiling among men beneath the cheerful light of the sun,'— the Sheol, of which Job said, 'I shall rest in desolate places, among kings and counsellors of old.' You were thinking, as they did, of the second life *of the soul only*,— a thought that lays a heavier weight upon the spirit than even that of annihilation. How much has the human heart gained in the One revelation, which enables it to say, 'I believe in the resurrection of the body'; that gives the flesh also leave 'to rest in hope'! It is this belief which brings with it all that is actual and personal into our future life; all, too, that is homely and familiar; that gives us back our friends, looking and talking as they did here; gives us back our feelings and occupations, in fact, our lives. For the body is, after all, the home of the soul, endeared, even like the actual home, by the very sorrows that have been endured within it; and we can conceive of nothing entered upon in separation from it that is worthy to be called life. When I think of death, it is never as setting the soul free from the body, but rather as admitting it into a state where these two, in the marriage of the purified soul with the glorified body, will learn the true blessedness of their union, all being removed that has sometimes made it irksome and constraining.

"And thus it has not been in seasons of weariness and despondency that the thought of death has been the sweetest to me; but at times, when my whole nature has been the most keenly strung to enjoyment, there has come within my soul a longing, an aching wish to be more in the heart of the beauty which encompasses but does not touch it; a desire 'not *to be unclothed, but clothed upon*, that mortality may be swallowed up in life.' Do you know anything of that feeling of sadness and disquietude peculiar to the depth of summer; something which will not let the heart rest in the midst of the fulness and stillness that surrounds it, but weighs it down with a sense of strain and oppression, as if it were hard for it to respond to the full and joyful note which nature then strikes? It is not only the renewed spirit that reaches out after something *far better* than is here to be attained; there is a fulness of natural as well as of spiritual joy not yet wholly given. We have nothing to draw with, *yet the well is deep*, and man's heart and his flesh cry out for the living God: they claim the resurrection you speak of; they ask to see life, the whole of life bloom, as a flower, according to the fancy of the old alchemists, might be revived from its ashes.

"And is it not some instinct of this resurrection that lends such an intimate charm to all that gives oneness to life? There is nothing in our nature more religious than that which binds life consciously together, the power of Association; the full strength and sweetness of its deep conservatism can be only known, I think, to pure lives, whose very ghosts are comfortable, to loving spirits that have been faithful to the treasure committed to them, even if it be but to the 'few things' of their earliest days. Also, I think its power is best felt in lives that have been so far happy that they have known no violent wrench or dislocation, no blight, leaving some wide space unfruitful for the after harvest, so that the wealthy soul, 'enriched unto bountifulness,' may bring forth out of its treasure things new and old. *Life is one;* therefore it is well that childhood and youth should be happy; every life should begin in Eden; should have its blest traditions to return to, its holy places on which an eternal consecration rests. The dew of the birth of each most hallowed, most human thought and impulse within us is of the womb of the morning, and there is surely a literal meaning in our Saviour's words, 'Unless ye become like little children, ye cannot *enter* the kingdom of heaven.' The moments that set its doors widest open show us this; at times, when the great unseen world is nearest to us, the thought of childhood will return, and at the sound of the everlasting ocean, we stoop down to pick up the shells we used then to play with. When a great happiness floods our life, and lifts it far above its accustomed level, it sets it down upon no peak or summit of ecstasy, but brings us upon its wave some childish, trivial joy, some fondly recollected pleasure; it fills the heart with the sunshine of some long, golden afternoon of holiday, or with the fireside warmth of some long-deserted parlor. Do you remember how Joan of Arc, when crowned at Rheims, sees the kind, homely faces of her sisters in the crowd, and is at once carried back to the green valley, the silent mountain, the free simplicity of her early days? All that she has attained since then seems dream and shadow. 'The evening and the morning make our day.'"

"The homeliest associations," said Philip, "are ever those that have in them the most of tenderness. No passage in Holy Scripture has ever seemed to me more affecting than those words used by the Evangelist in describing our Saviour's garments at the Transfiguration: '*Whiter than any fuller on earth can whiten.*' The simplicity of the allusion seems to bring that majestic, unearthly scene, with all its overwhelming associations, into unity with our daily life; it knits and weaves together the every-day and the everlasting, and bids us

> 'Live
> In reconcilement with our stinted powers,
> . . . . . and seek
> *For present good in life's familiar face,*
> And build thereon our hopes of good to come.'

"How often have I felt a sacred power in the common things of life! They set a limit to thoughts that are too vast and oppressive for our mortal nature, and tend, in some way which I cannot analyze, to connect our personal identity with the eternal existence of God. I have known moments when they have become sacramental to me; when they have seemed to bring God before me as a tender parent, whose mercies are over all his works. How often is he made known to us in the breaking of bread; revealed through some slight circumstance; made manifest under some familiar aspect! I remember, last year, when I was recovering from a fever, lying one evening between sleeping and waking, too weak and restless to command my thoughts, which drifted out far beyond every known boundary into that dark, confused, *diffused* idea of God, in which he is at once everywhere and nowhere. Gently, gradually, I was drawn back by the low tones of my mother and sister pleasantly talking over some little household incidents in the fire-light; their gentle, subdued voices seemed to change the world from the void and chaos of nature into my Father's house; they led my spirit into His Presence who rejoices in the *habitable* parts of the earth, and makes his delight in the sons of men.

"And how friendly," he continued, "to our

higher nature are all things that are simple, kindly, *homely*, as opposed to such as are factitious and conventional. Artificial tastes and pleasures can never either cheer or refresh the heart; they have no root within our true life; they are not of the Father, but of the world. How sweet and wholesome are the pleasures that go into small room; the humble, simple, accustomed sights and sounds that bring the soul at once into the open air. Some of these are at all times full of deep suggestions, of quiet, unspoken recognitions, filling the heart with unspeakable tranquillity and peace. All that has to do with rural occupations, — haymaking and harvesting, the cheerful bustle and cackle of a farm-yard, the breath of cows, the broad, slanting light of evening, the wide glitter of a meadow in an autumn morning, and neither last nor least, the aspect of a cottage kitchen in the afternoon, with 'all things in order stored,' — these things fill me with a sense of the Fatherhood of God — "

"Such," I said, "as you would gain from some passage in the New Testament, where

Christ makes himself a partaker of flesh and blood, through his gracious condescension to the humble requirements, the lowly solaces our nature claims; as when at the wedding-feast he turns the water into wine, and stoops down at the last supper to wash the feet of his disciples."

"And yet," returned Philip, musingly, "is Christ indeed a friend to the region we have been speaking of, — a friend, I mean, who *shows himself* friendly? Sometimes it seems to me as if he would at the last be generous to all that is in itself excellent; that he will yet stoop down and recognize some of the fair and fading flowers of humanity that he now passes by without a glance; that he will breathe upon them and bid them be ever-blooming. Yet the silence of the New Testament is a wonderful thing. Love, except of a spiritual kind, is never mentioned there. Outward nature, of which the Old Testament is so full, scarcely brought in, even as the background of the scene filled up with man's deeper and immortal destinies. Where in these pages is the world, — the world that goes on around us, and we along with it; the world of feeling, of endeavor, of hope, of wearying care and bitter anguish; 'this world, troublesome and yet beloved,' that we do not, cannot escape from until we have done with it forever? And when I think upon these things," he added, "an oblique light seems cast upon what has long seemed strangely certain to me, that Christianity should tend not only, as you say, to separation, but also to narrowness. It is easy to be wise upon the mistakes of religious people, to say that they miss the broad and loving character of the Gospel, straitening it to their own minds; but it is not so easy to account for some constantly reappearing signs of a limited mode of viewing nature and life, such as over-strictness in the education of the young, and a strained disapproval of amusement, so evidently a part of man, that it may, under its more favorable conditions, be literally termed his *re*-creation. Nor is it yet easy to account for what it would be vain to deny, that, looking at things on a broader scale, the spiritual basis has ever proved too weak to bear up the whole man. How narrow, how little *human*, has been in all ages the *merely* religious world! And how largely has that very world benefited by movements exterior, and even antagonistic to it; as when the revival of the Greek and Latin literature brought a fresh breath over Christendom. Mere spirituality seems to exhaust the soil that rears it, so that Christianity must always gain much from extraneous sources. It does so, in our own day, from science and general social progress. These are its friends, though sometimes disguised ones; and Christ still gathers where he did not straw, and reaps where he did not sow."

"But are you so sure," I said, "that Christ has not strawed and sown in these very fields? Christ is the light of the world as well as the light of his Church. He is a Man, One to whom nothing that Humanity endures or achieves can be alien, so that it seems less strange to me that some of the greatest conquests of the truth should have been won *for* the Church and not by it, — that so many rich acquisitions, take, for instance, that of religious toleration, should have fallen into it through the gradual progress of human enlightenment. The Church and the world must grow together, — they *do* grow together, though they cannot as yet grow in harmony; suffering from the world's enmity, suffering still more from its friendship, straitened on all sides, the Church has become straitened in herself, timid and distrustful, as that which is in antagonism must ever be. In all that concerns Christianity under its present dispensation, we must be prepared to meet with a certain degree of check and disappointment. We find it even in Christ himself; he will now be loved for his own sake, be followed in his silence and severity; he will still give a present contradiction to many of the heart's most fair and cherished ideals, just as his earthly coming in poverty and humiliation contradicted the Jewish idea of the Messianic world-dominion, *yet this was a true idea*, and one which Christ will yet abundantly fulfil. And if the Christ of the New Testament does not, as you say, meet and satisfy all the demands of our nature, — if it does not answer to the whole man, is it not because it does not give us the whole Christ? Where in the four Gospels shall we find the Messiah, full of glory, majesty, and terror, red in his apparel, travelling in the greatness of his strength, the King of righteousness and peace, the Lord and Giver of earthly fulness and felicity, binding his foal to the vine and his ass's colt to the choice vine? Are we not slow to receive *all* that the Psalms and the prophets have spoken concerning HIM? Wolff, if you remember, says that the error of the Jews of old did not lie, as we often deem, in looking to Christ as the founder of a temporal kingdom, but in failing to recognize him under the humiliation which was foretold as to precede its establishment. For this want of recognition our Lord himself rebukes his disciples, when he says to them, '*Ought* not Christ to have suffered these things, and then to have entered into his glory?' And as regards present times, Wolff tells us that he was never able to make any way in argument with his own people until he freely admitted to them *that the Messiah had yet to come.* 'At what time,' they would ask, 'has the Christian Church seen the fulfilment of prophecies such as those of the 11th of Isaiah and the 72d Psalm?' "

"True," said Philip, "there is nothing historical in these passages of Scripture, nor yet in that remarkable series of Psalms, beginning at the 95th, which have been, with the 100th, in which they culminate, considered as forming *one* grand prophetic poem, celebrating the majesty and righteousness of Christ's kingdom on earth. Their cry is still, '*He cometh, he cometh* to judge the world in righteousness, and the people with his truth.' "

"And with Christ's second coming," I said, "as the Restorer of all things, is evidently linked the conversion and restitution of the Jewish people; '*when* the Lord shall build up Zion, he shall appear in his glory.' This connection is brought out so clearly in the Old Testament, that it seems strange that Christians can continually read it, and still persist in taking the magnificent promises, of which Isaiah, Zechariah, and all the lesser prophets are so full, in their spiritual regenerative aspect *only*, when their plain literal meaning is one which does not drop off like a husk at the unfolding of their spiritual import, but expands along with it, growing like a double fruit upon the same stalk, *so that neither can ripen fully until both do.* Christ is to be a Light to lighten the Gentiles, and to be *the glory* of his people Israel; the same Hour (so speaks prophetic testimony) that brings in Israel's conversion, will bring in man's full reconciliation with God. The veil which overspreads all nations rests as yet upon the eyes of Israel, and upon the heart of the Gentile Church, 'yet in *this* mountain, in Zion,' saith God, 'it shall be taken away'; a promise initially fulfilled in the day of Pentecost, but to receive a yet fuller accomplishment in the Day when God returns to Jerusalem with mercies. That day will be one of rich ingathering. 'Great,' saith the Prophet Hosea, 'shall be the day of Jezreel'; Jezreel, a name combining terror with mercy, meaning at once 'I will scatter' and 'I will sow.' God will sow by them whom he has scattered; and it is certain that the Jews will be in an eminent degree the Evangelists of the Second Dispensation, as they were of the First."

"It is an office," said Philip, "for which they will be in many ways peculiarly fitted. Called into the vineyard at the Eleventh Hour, they have not, like the Christian Church, borne the long day's heat and burden; nor will they have, like it, a time-engendered acrimony, caused by the sharp separation of opinion, to contend with. Do you remember the passage in Wolff's *Autobiography*, where he tells us of his going up Mount Sinai to pray for the whole Church of God; for the noble Stolberg and the other Roman Catholic friends of his early life, endeared through so many kindly associations; for Mr. Drummond and all his beloved English friends and fellow-helpers in the work of Christ; and for his own people, those kinsfolk, '*to whom pertaineth the promises*, whose are the fathers, and of whom concerning the flesh Christ came'? God hath not cast away his people whom he foreknew; their faith, when it is once enlightened to receive Christ, will have a character of its own; it will be childlike, implicit, and objective. It must be easy, I think, and *natural* for a Jew to look to God as a father; all their ancient ideas of him, whether of severity or love, are fatherly; he is even 'the Father of the dew': one who takes all creation under his individual superintendence. So that to them, in a peculiar manner, belong the fruition of all those rich *earthly* and yet evangelic promises, into which the Christian Church, baptized into *the death* of her beloved Lord, and cradled in suffering and strife, has as yet scarcely entered. It must wait for the companionship of the reconciled Elder Brother, then there will be dancing and music; 'music in the heart, music in the house,' — in the whole great united household."

"The Messianic promises," I said, "are indeed earthly; they are of the earth, as the rose and the lily are, and yet not 'earthy'; there is no grave-damp about them, no odor of corruptibility. What picture can be conceived by the human imagination more lovely than that scene portrayed in the eighth chapter of Zechariah, where all the finer affections of our nature find room and time for expansion, where the heart enjoys its long-desolated Sabbaths! Here, the ground gives her increase, and the heavens their dew; 'in the streets of Jerusalem old men and old women dwell, and every man with his staff in his hand *for very age*'; while the same streets are 'full of boys and girls playing'; and the still remembered fasts of the Old Covenant are 'turned into joy and gladness, and cheerful feasts.' And we must not fail to remark, that this period of unexampled temporal felicity is also one of extraordinary * spiritual illumination, a time of prayer, of intercession, of holy activity; a time when God dwells in the midst of his people; a time of intimate correspondence between earth and heaven. When God says in Hosea, 'I will hear the heavens, and they shall hear the earth,' he says also, '*And the earth shall hear the corn, and the wine, and the oil.*' It is easy to decry the literal interpretation of prophecy as carnal and limited; easy to ask, what better shall we be for hills of corn and

* Zechariah viii. 19, *seq.*

barley, and for mountains dropping sweet wine? but who can look into the world as it now is, without admitting how true, how heaven-sent a blessing material abundance would be, were that within man which is inimical to its true enjoyment once taken away? It is only human selfishness that makes good things evil to us; the richest boon the Father can send carries no sorrow with it to hearts that are prepared to share it as brethren. Even as we live and feel now, 'comfort,' which is too often a selfish and hardening thing, may become an evangelic one. The spirit of the world is one which makes a great feast, and invites *many* to it, but gives no kiss to the individual guest, — does not anoint his head with oil, brings him no water for his feet; but do you not know houses where a refined attention to bodily comfort seems but the expression of an inward cordiality, — houses where a sort of physical *bien-être* prevails, where a genial soul makes its presence felt like that of the summer sunshine, or the winter hearth, so that your very food seems to do you more good than it does elsewhere? In the late accounts of the work of the Bible-women in London, the poor women who are sometimes invited to pass an evening at the Mission-room seem to derive as much benefit from the kind looks and gentle voices of the ladies, from the good tea, the good fire, the flowers set upon the table, the unaccustomed luxury of a quiet room, as from anything they gain in the way of direct instruction. In all these things there is a tenderness that goes to the very soul."

"Yes," said Philip, "and that does not depart from it quickly. There are some whom I have known on earth, who are now departed from it, that I find it difficult to think of, even in heaven, under any other aspect than that of ministering, welcoming, making every one around them comfortable, though I know not what form their tender, ever active solicitude may take where there are none weary, or sick, or sorrowful, where there are no strangers to be entertained, no wayfarers to be cheered and comforted."

Philip was silent; at this moment a sudden smile came out over the sky and sea, that seemed like an answer to our unspoken thoughts. O, what did it not recall; what did it not promise! The glory of the terrestrial and of the celestial in one! Memory and Hope, that met and kissed each other in the thought of partings that had been rich in a heavenly foretaste, in the anticipation of meetings that would be more tender than even the partings of earth!

> "There was no cloud, no flaming bar, no line
> Of fire along the west, but solemnly
> Heaven glowed unto its depths, as if the curse
> Were lifted upwards from our universe
> One moment's Sabbath space, and only love
> Stooped down above its world! — so from above
> A smile dropt visibly on earth, that prest
> To meet that sign of reconcilement, blest
> On brow and bosom, blest."

Philip was the first to speak. "How Nature can sometimes hide her deep, original wound! Where, at such a moment as this, is the faint undergroaning of creation?"

"Yet surely," I said, "it is in such moments as these that the heart puts in its strongest claim for the promised restitution of all things. When Nature hides her wound, she does but *hide* it, and of this the soul is conscious. When her smile is the kindest, the heart feels that she can but smile; she has no healing balm to pour, no life-giving Word to speak. She has, it is true, a ministry for man, but in it there is nothing priestly, no laver of regenerating purity, no chrism of absolving love. Her house is the house of bondage, out of which she can never lead man's spirit, *for Nature herself needs to be redeemed.* Science has taught us that discord was *not* introduced into creation by man, nor did it follow, as it is usual to suppose, in consequence of his disobedience; the revelations of geology prove abundantly that pain and death reigned from the beginning, therefore is it that the Cross must go so deep. Christ must subdue this kingdom also, must deliver it up to God,* even to the Father, *and until then* Christ's own kingdom remains a kingdom of patience and of subjection. His word, one of separation, sharper than that of any two-edged sword, and the Christian life, one in which there is ever a foreseen death,

* 1 Cor. xv. 24.

the sacrifice of the human will, '*even the death of the cross.*'"

"And are you," said Philip, "led to believe that this separation will go on through the whole of the present dispensation, becoming ever more and more definite? The final victory of good is the one great certainty of the believing heart; and our natural feelings lead us to expect that this victory will be gradual and progressive; an expectation, however, which is *not* confirmed by prophecy, which leads us rather to contemplate the two kingdoms of good and evil, each increasing, strengthening themselves against each other before a great concluding struggle, out of which good will rise triumphant and jubilant? A friend has asked me, 'Will not good and evil, before this final shock, draw more widely apart, and become *compact?* Good, through the building up of Christ's body, and the closer mutual adhesion of his scattered members; Evil, also standing up incarnate in the person of Antichrist?'"

"There is surely," I said, "something of

this gradual separation revealed in the deepened moral consciousness of the days we live in. Our eyes seem opened to discern between good and evil; those who now prefer the latter, do so knowingly and consciously. We can hardly, as even worthy people were wont to be in the generation which is passing from us, be *amused* with books and representations which draw their zest from the exhibition of sin and folly. We feel that there is in these things the nature and the power of death; and the spirit of levity, even though it occupy a large space in our literature, seems foreign to it, and not to belong to our present order. Even the intellect of our day revolts from the shallow systems that are now afloat, — afloat truly, and drifting on the surface of the age, for they have no root within its heart and life, such, I mean, as tend to minimize the strength and depth and vitality of sin. Whether they choose to represent it as a lower undeveloped form of good, a thing transmutable, *with no essence of its own*, or as being merely the want of balance and proportion, a question of too much or too little in the poising of man's nature, only needing readjustment, they have but one practical effect, and that is, to eat the heart out of our whole spiritual life; to make even the life of Christ, the truest life that has ever lived, to make even his dying, a sort of drama. If there is no reality in sin, what becomes of the deep reality of sacrifice? *To what need was this great cost?*

"And what is there in Scripture which favors the idea of any gradual absorption of evil? Isaiah, a book stored with evangelic comfort, *concludes* with a denunciation on this point, the awfulness of which cannot be surpassed by human language; and is there not something deeply significant in a fact which the so-called adherents of 'Jesus, not Paul,' would do well to consider, that it is from our Lord's own lips (and this, I think, without a solitary exception) that the severest warnings of future judgment fall. He it is, and not any one apostle, who speaks of the fire unquenchable, the worm that never dies; he who describes, under many similitudes, the final separation between the good and evil, and the utter rejection of the latter. Good and evil are antagonistic independent powers, separate from the beginning, separate even unto the end. What communion hath Christ with Belial? what fellowship hath light with darkness? Milton has taught us to look upon the Devil as a fallen angel, a being originally good; yet we are told by St. John, and by One greater than he, that he was a liar and a murderer *from the beginning.* This is a subject which surely does not invite to a vague sentimentalism. Who can trace the history of the past? who can read the history of the present? who, in other words, can take up a newspaper and refuse to believe in the existence of a dark kingdom of fraud, and cruelty, and unspeakable iniquity underlying the superficial prosperity of our daily life; a kingdom that draws its strength and allurement from a spiritual source, *a kingdom that hath foundations,* — foundations which are being continually more and more laid bare by the Light which shall at last triumph over them, as completely as the glory of the sunshine now fills every nook and crevice of some giant ruin that once resounded to the shout of '*Ave Cæsar, morituri te salutant.*'"

"A cry," said Philip, "which, translated into a purer language, has now become the watchword of the soldier and servant of Christ. It seems to me that in no other age of the world has the attraction of the Cross been so deeply felt as it is in this, — perhaps because it has been never so much needed as it is now to explain the dark parables of nature; the grievous contradictions of life. It is certain that the primitive Church, though it lived beneath its shadow, clasped it less closely to the heart than we do. Simplicity and cheerfulness are the leading characteristics of the pictures in the Catacombs. It is remarkable that the Cross does not appear in them, nor any figure that tends to show a strong consciousness of sin, and the corresponding sense of alienation from God. Here we have Christ, the King, the good Shepherd, *ever with his book*, in the midst of his faithful ones in earth and heaven, between which two places there is no division apparent except that of Jordan, — for so is death represented, — a slender, easily-crossed stream, the opposite banks distinguishable by the thorns and snares on one side, and the ever-blooming flowers on the other. The two pervading, continually recurring ideas are those of the guardianship of Christ, '*Ego sum pastor bonus*,' and of the Resurrection, brought out over and again under the favorite type of Jonah. This infant, blood-baptized Church, deeply suffering, was not, it seems, so deeply sorrowing as ours; it did not know our intellectual sadness, our doubts, our weariness, our worldliness, our strifes among brethren. The star Wormwood had not then fallen, making all the waters of the earth bitter."

"And yet," I said, "were they to become exceeding bitter, so that no man could drink them, *the Lord hath showed us a Tree.*"

"Beneath thy Cross I stand,
Jesus, my Saviour, turn and look on me!
O, who are these that, one on either hand,
Are crucified with thee?

"The one that turns away
With sullen, scoffing lip, and one whose eyes

Close o'er the words, 'Yet shalt thou be this day
With me in Paradise.'

"Here would I fain behold
This twofold mystery, Love's battle won,
Its warfare ended, and its ransom told,
Its conquest but begun!

"I say not to thee now,
Come from the Cross and then will I believe;
O, lift me up to thee, and teach me how
To love and how to grieve.

"I tracked thy footsteps long;
For where thou wert, there would thy servant be;
But now, methought the silence, now the throng,
Would part me still from thee.

"I sought thee 'mid the leaves,
I found thee on the dry and blasted tree;
I saw thee not until I saw the thieves
There crucified with thee!"

Cambridge : Stereotyped and Printed by Welch, Bigelow, & Co.

www.ingramcontent.com/pod-product-compliance
Lightning Source LLC
LaVergne TN
LVHW011236110826
845150LV00006B/1652